Family Violence

Look for these and other books in the Lucent Overview series:

Abortion	Homeless Children
Acid Rain	Illegal Immigration
Alcoholism	Illiteracy
Animal Rights	Immigration
Artificial Organs	Mental Illness
The Beginning of Writing	Money
The Brain	Ocean Pollution
Cancer	Oil Spills
Censorship	The Olympic Games
Child Abuse	Organ Transplants
Cities	Ozone
The Collapse of the Soviet Union	Pesticides
Dealing with Death	Police Brutality
Death Penalty	Population
Democracy	Prisons
Drug Abuse	Rainforests
Drugs and Sports	Recycling
Drug Trafficking	The Reunification of Germany
Eating Disorders	Schools
Endangered Species	Smoking
The End of Apartheid in South Africa	Space Exploration
Energy Alternatives	Special Effects in the Movies
Espionage	Teen Alcoholism
Euthanasia	Teen Pregnancy
Extraterrestrial Life	Teen Suicide
Family Violence	The UFO Challenge
Gangs	The United Nations
Garbage	The U.S. Congress
Gay Rights	The U.S. Presidency
The Greenhouse Effect	Vanishing Wetlands
Gun Control	Vietnam
Hate Groups	World Hunger
Hazardous Waste	Zoos
The Holocaust	

Family Violence

by Liza N. Burby

LUCENT
BOOKS

LUCENT *Overview Series*

Library of Congress Cataloging-in-Publication Data

Burby, Liza N.
    Family violence / Liza N. Burby.
        p.   cm. — (Lucent overview series)
    Includes bibliographical references and index.
    Summary: Examines issues related to child abuse, battered
wives, and other family violence concerns and what can be done
about them.
    ISBN 1-56006-173-1 (alk. paper)
    1. Family violence—Juvenile literature.   [1. Family violence.]
I. Title.   II. Series.
HQ809.B87   1996
362.82'92—dc20   95-25108
                                            CIP
                                            AC

Contents

Introduction

VIOLENCE AGAINST children and women was once an acceptable part of family life. Men and women did not think of their abusive behavior as wrong; indeed, actions like beating and hitting were sanctioned by laws that everyone followed to enforce discipline within their families.

In colonial America, for example, "stubborn children laws" made it legal for the male head of a household to beat his children to death if he thought them too unruly. A husband had the freedom to pull his wife's hair, choke her, spit in her face, and kick her. The law also allowed him to beat her with a stick, provided it was no thicker than his thumb.

Public sympathies

But in 1874, two events occurred that began to change public opinion about the acceptable treatment of children and women. The first involved ten-year-old Mary Ellen Wilson, who was discovered starving and chained to her bed in a New York City tenement apartment. As no child protection agency yet existed, the Society for the Prevention of Cruelty to Animals had her removed from her adoptive parents' care.

The incident aroused public sympathies and led to the creation of the New York City Society

(Opposite page) A mother and child march with other protesters in Harlem, N.Y., to draw attention to the serious problem of family violence. As public awareness of abuse increases so does society's effort to end it.

for the Prevention of Cruelty to Children, still in operation today. Also in response, child protection groups sprang up in all major cities, focused especially on the welfare of children living in poverty. Various child abuse laws were passed, but few of them were effective because there was no system in place for reporting child abuse. Even when a person was aware that a child was being abused, he or she did not know whom to tell about it. Therefore, most often, the child did not get help and the abuse continued.

Second, in 1874, a North Carolina court became the first to rule against "wife-whipping." However, the court did not open the door for women who had been battered to file complaints against their spouses. Instead, it ruled that as the woman involved had not been permanently injured and the husband had shown no malice, it was "better to draw the curtain, shut out the public gaze, and leave the parties to forgive and forget." In other words, a man should not hit his wife, but if he did, it was no one's business but his own.

Decade of governmental intervention

This state of affairs remained unchanged for another century. People recognized that child abuse could be a problem, but little was done to stop it until 1962, when C. Henry Kempe, a Denver pediatrician, published an article entitled "The Battered-Child Syndrome." This influential article forced people to acknowledge that child abuse was a serious problem. Kempe asserted that many children arriving in hospital emergency rooms with mysterious bruises and broken bones had been abused by someone who was caring for them. He explained that X rays can clearly show when a child has been beaten on a regular basis. And Kempe and four colleagues admitted:

"Physicians, because of their own feelings . . . may have great reluctance in believing that parents were guilty of abuse." Kempe urged doctors to pay more attention to children's bruises and injuries so that doctors could detect whether the injury was the result of abuse, and get the children the help they needed.

Through the ongoing work of Kempe and others, the 1970s became the decade of governmental intervention. Congress passed the Child Abuse Prevention and Treatment Act in 1974, establishing the first program to collect information and record statistics of child abuse and neglect. The act also sponsored programs to prevent, identify, and treat child abuse.

Today a system of laws and agencies is in place designed to aid children who have been abused. Now when someone suspects that a child is being hurt by a caretaker, he or she can contact child protective services, nationwide, for help.

A family matter

The 1970s was a decade of action for abused women, too. As part of the women's rights movement, activists attempted to publicize the problem of abuse of women by their husbands and boyfriends. They organized shelters or safe houses for women who were running away from their abusive partners. They also lobbied for legislation that could protect abused women.

But even so, the curtain rule of 1874 seemed to thrive. In 1975, 101 years after that decision, a Washington, D.C., man with a history of violence against his wife broke three bones in her face. She reported him to the police and a judicial hearing was scheduled. But a superior court judge would not let the case go to court. Instead, he held a private meeting with the husband and wife. He later told a reporter: "This is the best way to

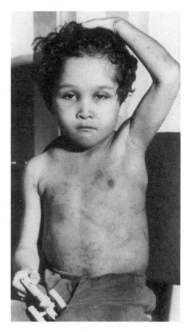

When this photo of a boy who was abused by his stepfather was taken in 1959, little was done to stop family violence. Many people viewed abusive behavior as an acceptable part of family life or as a family's private matter.

Protesters on the Capitol Mall in Washington, D.C., rally against domestic violence. As society becomes more aware of the widespread and complex problem of family violence, misconceptions about child abuse and spousal abuse have begun to erode.

handle this type of situation. This is a family matter. They can settle this without airing a lot of dirty linen."

As author Maria Roy writes in her 1977 book, *Battered Women: A Psychosociological Study of Domestic Violence*, through the ages someone has always been "settling the matter by drawing the curtain, shutting out the public gaze, and deciding not to air a lot of dirty linen."

Socially unacceptable behavior

In the past twenty years, as public awareness of child abuse and spouse abuse continues to grow, these attitudes toward family violence have changed. While there are extreme examples of people who still believe they have a right to use violence against a family member, most people recognize that physical abuse of anyone is wrong. Violence directed toward any family member has been against the law for the last ten years. As for changes in the actual incidence of violence, Sharon Herzberger, a psychology professor at Trinity College in Connecticut, told the author:

> When people ask if family violence is decreasing, if you look at the long view, one hundred years ago, when people killed family members all the time, then you could say it is decreasing. In shorter time periods, it's hard to tell. We pay more attention to family violence today. But now it is harder to get anyone to admit doing it. They recognize that it is socially unacceptable.

As society is more willing to expose matters once considered private, misconceptions about family violence will slowly erode. Terry Bordan, a certified mental health counselor in New York, believes that society now knows that family violence is wrong, that it now knows how to detect signs that someone is being abused, that it even knows how to report suspected violence and how to activate programs that can help victims and their abusers. The one thing that remains to be discovered, Bordan says, is a way to prevent the violence from occurring in the first place. Until that happens, family violence will continue to be a major societal problem.

1

The Scope of Family Violence

A HOME IS A HAVEN from the rest of the world. It is a place in which children and adults expect to feel safe; a place in which life should be stable, loving, and free of major crises. Yet sometimes that sense of security is violated. Behind many closed doors parents hurt their children with cruel words and strong fists. Some men and women harm each other in equally terrible and violent ways. Sometimes this violence leads to death. These behaviors define a societal problem known as family violence.

Statistics indicate that family violence is a grave problem that shows no sign of going away. The Centers for Disease Control and Prevention (CDC) in Atlanta has declared family violence the number one public health problem, because it affects not only a person's physical health, but also his or her psychological well-being. Secretary of Health and Human Services Donna Shalala has repeatedly warned that family violence is an unacknowledged epidemic in our society.

What is family violence?

Sometimes family violence is referred to as intimate violence because the victim and the abuser

(Opposite page) Harmed by those who are supposed to love and care for them, abused children and adults often feel unsafe in their own home. This betrayal of trust can make them feel helpless and alone.

13

are closely related. Many different terms are used to describe family violence, including battering, spouse abuse, domestic violence, and child abuse.

Family violence involves family members who are supposed to love and trust each other, from infants to parents to grandparents, and who become victims of another family member who intentionally hurts them. Violence can be physical, psychological, or sexual. Physical violence is any act by a person that causes pain or injury. Such acts can include hitting with a fist, stick, strap, or any hard object; frequently, common household items from a frying pan to an ice pick become weapons. Often the violence includes pushing, shoving, grabbing, kicking, and biting. This abuse can cause broken bones; concussions; permanent brain damage; hearing loss; and miscarriages, or the loss of a pregnancy.

A fearful environment

According to psychology professor Sharon Herzberger, in most cases of physical abuse the mistreatment is not a constant activity. The abuse can be sporadic, occurring once a day, once a week, or even once in a while. However, once someone has been abused the threat of the next attack serves just as effectively in creating a continuously fearful environment as a punch would. This leads to psychological violence, a condition that exists when one family member threatens to injure another or forces the other to perform degrading or humiliating acts. Sometimes the abuser isolates the victim from friends or family members who could help him or her.

Sexual violence includes rape or forced sex. It can occur in marriage or between siblings, a child and parent, or other live-in family members. When it involves family members other than two spouses, sexual violence is also known as incest.

Violence within families occurs between brothers and sisters, husbands and wives, parents and children, children and their elderly parents, and grandchildren and grandparents. But statistics indicate that the most frequent victims are children under the age of five and women involved in intimate relationships, either with a boyfriend or a husband. Though men have been abused by their wives and girlfriends, research has shown that 95 percent of the time women are the victims.

The youngest victims

About 1.5 million children, fifteen of every thousand, are seriously abused each year in the United States by a parent or guardian. In April 1995, the National Committee to Prevent Child Abuse reported that nearly 1,300 children had died from abuse the year before. Young children are at high risk for being killed during an abusive attack. Eighty-eight percent of these children were under the age of five, while an alarming 46 percent of these were under the age of one when they died.

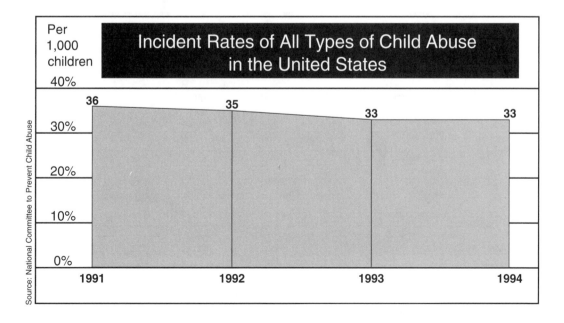

Incident Rates of All Types of Child Abuse in the United States

Source: National Committee to Prevent Child Abuse

Per 1,000 children

	1991	1992	1993	1994
	36	35	33	33

What makes this age group so vulnerable is their dependence on the abuser, explains certified mental health counselor Terry Bordan. She told the author:

> This is an age in which children are unable to care for themselves and must rely on their parents for all of their needs. Their parents may have unrealistic ideas about what their kids can do and they may place unfair demands on them, like they can never cry or they have to take care of their parents. Also, little kids, especially babies, are physically unable to protect themselves.

The incidence of violence against children appears to be on the upswing. According to the National Committee to Prevent Child Abuse, from 1976, when the first national figures for child abuse were collected, to 1990, reports of abuse grew from 416,033 per year to 1,700,000 per year. Data from the National Research Council do not indicate if the increase means there is actually

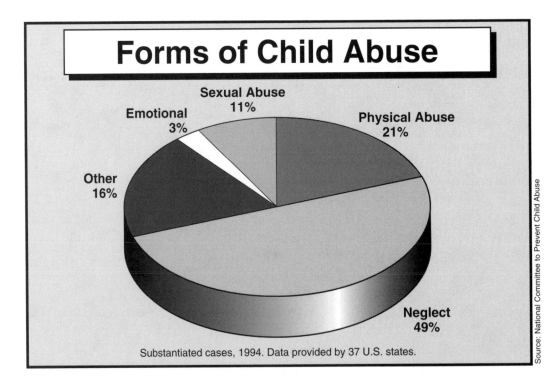

Forms of Child Abuse

Sexual Abuse 11%

Emotional 3%

Physical Abuse 21%

Other 16%

Neglect 49%

Substantiated cases, 1994. Data provided by 37 U.S. states.

Source: National Committee to Prevent Child Abuse

A battered woman seeks safety at a New York soup kitchen. Considered a true epidemic by the American Medical Association, domestic violence affects millions of women each year.

more violence or if people are simply reporting violence more often, but Bordan says that social workers and emergency room technicians who work directly with victims believe they may be witnessing a rise in the violence itself.

Battered women

Violence against women is also a serious and escalating problem. Battering is the single most common cause of injury to women, exceeding muggings, motor vehicle accidents, and workplace injuries combined. The CDC says that between 2 and 4 million women across the country are battered each year. The American Medical Association has declared domestic violence against women a true epidemic, one that kills an estimated 2,000 to 4,000 women each year. Further, it is the number one cause of emergency room visits for women. By some estimates, as many as one-third to one-fifth of all women who visit emergency rooms are victims of abuse by their husbands or boyfriends. Spouse abuse leads to almost 100,000 days of hospitalization, 30,000 emergency room visits, and 40,000 trips to the doctor each year.

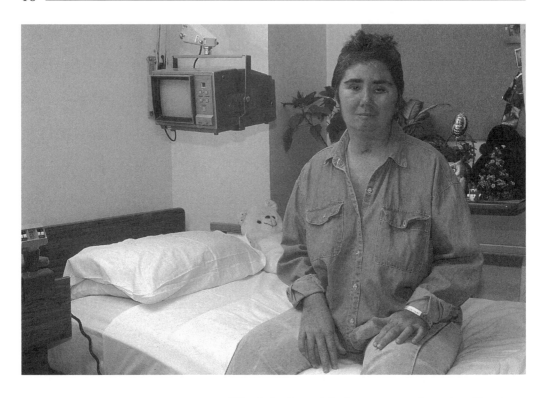

A woman whose boyfriend hit her with a baseball bat after she tried to leave him sits in a hospital room after seeking treatment. Domestic violence accounts for most of the emergency room visits by women.

The injuries with the most serious implications may be those suffered by pregnant women, in particular. At least 240,000 are battered each year in the United States, which is about 6 percent of all pregnant women. In addition to miscarriages, battering can cause severe harm to the unborn child. The March of Dimes says that the number one cause of birth defects is abuse of pregnant women.

Women can be considered vulnerable to abuse for many of the same reasons as can children. Physically they are not as strong as men. A 110-pound woman is no physical match for a 220-pound man. Many are also dependent upon their partners for financial support, making it difficult for them to leave the relationship if they are abused. But the reasons that women become victims of abuse are actually much more complex. Joan Sculli, director of the Nassau County Coalition Against Domestic Violence, Inc., in New York, says, "For years researchers have been trying to find that one common denominator that makes a woman more vulnerable to abuse. It doesn't exist."

Sculli explains that violence against women usually occurs in relationships in which a man feels a need to control his partner and uses threatening and abusive behavior to do so. Ironically, batterers use abuse against a spouse as a powerful mechanism to cement the relationship, to hold on to it, not to destroy it. She told the author:

> The abuser is an individual who is using the threat of injury and pain as part of this pattern to control his partner's behavior. Usually the abuser is in a position to leave the relationship. If he didn't want it to exist, he could walk out on it. The dynamic is part of what confuses people because usually we don't think of using pain and suffering to hold on to a relationship.

This confusion extends to the myths and misinterpretations about who is abusive and who is most vulnerable to the abuse. Many people believe that domestic violence occurs only in poor, uneducated families. But family violence is not limited to any religious, social, or economic group. It involves people who are rich and poor, college educated and high school dropouts, of every race and religious belief.

Trapped by misconceptions

Christine Martell, who runs organizations in Massachusetts to help battered women, told the author that her misunderstanding about what kind of families violence can occur in trapped her in an abusive relationship. Martell, whose husband regularly threatened to shoot her during their three-year marriage, says:

> It took me a couple of years to realize that I was in a dangerous relationship. We were both college-

educated and very wealthy. I thought domestic violence only happened to poor, uneducated women. I had to break through a lot of stereotypes before I was able to get out of the relationship.

Misconceptions about who can abuse sometimes makes it difficult for outsiders, or even victims, to realize that abuse is taking place. Abusers do not look different than nonabusers. Batterers can be men who go to work every day and support their families. They appear to be upstanding members of their communities. Parents who abuse their children can be seen as good disciplinarians whose children are well behaved.

Families at risk

However, there are groups that are at heightened risk to abuse. For instance, children are often more vulnerable when their parents are poor and young. While violence occurs at all economic levels, the stress of financial problems can be a risk factor for violent behavior toward children.

This seventeen-year-old mother of two offers to help other teens cope with the difficulties of parenthood. Young parents, especially those who live with the stresses of poverty, are not always equipped to deal with the challenges of parenting, and are therefore at greater risk of abusing their children.

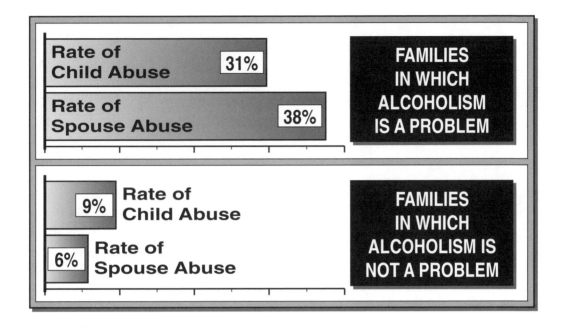

Rate of Child Abuse	31%	FAMILIES IN WHICH ALCOHOLISM IS A PROBLEM
Rate of Spouse Abuse	38%	
9% Rate of Child Abuse		FAMILIES IN WHICH ALCOHOLISM IS NOT A PROBLEM
6% Rate of Spouse Abuse		

While the age of a mother is not by itself an indicator of potential for violence, many mothers between the ages of fifteen and nineteen live in poverty. Many of them do not have a stable relationship with their young children's fathers. These young mothers may have a sense of frustration about having to care for a child, and may have no idea how to do so. For such mothers, clinicians say the rate of child abuse is particularly high, though definitive data have not been collected to date.

Families in which alcohol and drug abuse exist can also be at risk for family violence. When abuse occurs within a family, studies find that alcohol abuse and drug abuse were a factor approximately 51 percent of the time. Families in which alcoholism is a problem, in comparison to families in which it is not, show a much higher incidence of physical child abuse (31 percent to 9 percent) and spouse abuse (38 percent to 6 percent). Research indicates that while some abusers may use drinking as their excuse to be abusive, in partner abuse men with severe alcohol and drug problems are apt to abuse their partners whether they are drunk or not. They also inflict more serious injuries than do men who do not drink or take drugs, probably because of the loss of control associated with substance abuse. However, the research about this topic is still in the early stages.

Multiple abuses

Families can also be at high risk for multiple abuse. In families where violence occurs, often it involves many family members. Child abuse and spouse abuse have commonly been seen and treated as two separate problems. Though their histories are similar, only recently have psychologists begun to see how closely related the two really are. There is a misunderstanding that child abuse occurs independently from other family problems. This is actually rare. Children of battered women are also often at risk of being battered. The Family Violence Research Program at the University of New Hampshire indicates that about 810,000 abused children are living in households where spouse abuse also exists. A 1994 report from the National Clearinghouse for the Defense of Battered Women states that in approximately 50 percent of the households where there is spouse abuse, there is also child abuse.

According to a 1992 report issued by the National Council of Juvenile and Family Court Judges, child abuse usually begins after a pattern of wife abuse has been established. This abuse of the child by the battering man is likely to be serious. Seventy percent of the injuries inflicted on children by male batterers are severe, and 80 percent of child deaths within a family are caused by an abusive male. "The more severe the abuse of the mother, the worse the child abuse," says Barbara J.

Hart, managing attorney for the Pennsylvania Coalition Against Domestic Violence, and author of the report "State Codes on Domestic Violence, Analysis, Commentary, and Recommendations."

People who work with children say that even when physical abuse is not directed at the child, children are abused when they witness a parent being battered. A 1994 report, "The Impact of Domestic Violence on Children," by the American Bar Association states that children who witness abuse are harmed in several ways—cognitively, psychologically, and socially—merely by observing and hearing the abuse against a parent in their home. It is estimated that between 3.3 and 10 million children live in homes in which violence occurs. About 87 percent of those children witness that abuse.

Powerless to escape

Experts report that children's exposure to domestic violence can have immediate and traumatic effects. It can create fear for their own safety and for their mother's safety. It can also cause them to feel they are somehow to blame. They can develop concentration problems at school and they can also have trouble relating to peers.

Author Rosemary Bray, who saw her father abuse her mother, writes in the September/October 1994 issue of *Ms.* magazine:

> When we think about the toll domestic violence takes, we think first—and rightly so—about the women who are the targets of this violence. . . . But too often we forget about the silent witnesses to domestic terror, the children who grow up in violent homes. We understand that it's not good for them to see such a twisted version of male-female relationships. What we don't talk about is the profound effect a violent home has on the children who must live in it, people even more powerless to escape than their mothers.

Some people believe that a battered woman can protect her child from physical abuse or that the child is in less danger because the woman is the primary target of abuse. But this is not true. Battered women are in no position to protect their children from being abused by their husbands or boyfriends. Many of them suffer from low self-esteem. After many years of physical and emotional abuse, they may begin to suffer personality changes that can cause them to have unpredictable behavior. Many women become depressed, sometimes turning to drugs and alcohol. In short, their judgment and ability to care for their children might be impaired.

Nevertheless, the "failure to protect" section of child abuse statutes in forty-eight states concludes that when a parent does not act to protect his or her child, regardless of whether that person

Witnessing violence within the family can have immediate, traumatic, and long-lasting effects on a child.

is also being abused, he or she can be arrested. According to the National Council of Juvenile and Family Court Judges, in courts across the country battered women are frequently convicted of crimes or lose custody of their children on the grounds of failing to protect them.

Abused by their mothers

Unfortunately, when violence already exists in the family, battered mothers abuse their children in turn. More than half of abused women also use violence against their children. Reports from battered women's shelters, to which abused women run with their children to escape an abusive partner, indicate that even while women are in shelters and safe from attacks, they continue to abuse their children. The problem is such a serious one that most shelters have strict rules barring the use of physical punishment by women who live in them. In one Long Island, New York, shelter, a mother was given a warning the first time she struck her child. The second time, she was asked to leave the shelter and child protective services put her child in the care of a relative.

Sometimes children who live in homes in which violence exists are abused while trying to protect their mothers. According to Hart, in a 36-month study of 146 children, ages 11 to 17, who came from homes where wife beating was a major problem, all sons over the age of 14 attempted to protect their mothers and 62 percent of them were injured in the process.

Family violence rarely involves just two people. When abuse exists within a family, the whole family is scarred. Family violence is such a dangerous problem that it is recognized as a crime. But it is perhaps the only crime in the United States for which the perpetrator and the victim must share a home.

2

The Cycle of Violence

FAMILY VIOLENCE RARELY has a single cause. Those who work with abused children and intimate partners point to a combination of factors, not to any all-encompassing theory, as the root of abuse within families. But there appears to be one constant in most instances of family violence: Those who abuse family members either witnessed abuse or were abused as children. Thus begins a cycle in which violence leads to more violence. This observation found support in a 1993 study by the American Psychological Association seeking to determine the cause of violent behavior. The study found that the strongest predictor of violence is a history of violence within a family. Certified mental health counselor Terry Bordan explains:

> We do know that while not everyone who was abused becomes an abuser, everyone who abuses a child was himself abused. Therefore most such people don't see abuse as deviant or abnormal. Even when formerly abused people become abusers, they frequently have trouble controlling their behavior without some sort of intervention.

The cycle of violence is a behavioral pattern in which children who either witnessed abuse of a

(Opposite page) A history of family violence is a strong determinant of further violence in a family. This violence can affect many generations unless someone is able to break the cycle.

parent or a sibling or were themselves abused by a parent or other family member grow up to abuse their spouse, children, or both. Because it affects many generations of a family unless someone intervenes or someone tries to break the cycle, this pattern is also referred to as intergenerational violence.

Transmitted to another generation

A male child who witnesses spouse abuse by his father has a higher chance of growing up to be a wife abuser. More male batterers than female victims come from violent homes. Fully 80 percent of the male participants in a Minneapolis, Minnesota, violence-control program grew up in homes where they saw or were victims of physical, sexual, or other abuse. In fact, the majority of studies of abusive men find that a high percentage come from homes in which there was abuse of a spouse, a child, or both.

Mona Lou Callery, a former victim of spouse abuse who now counsels battered women in Massachusetts, says that her husband came from an abusive home. "We would really talk about the abuse sometimes," she explained to the author, "and he would describe what he had witnessed his father doing to his mother—and then the next beating I would get the same thing."

According to a 1992 domestic violence report compiled by Barbara J. Hart, managing attorney of the Pennsylvania Coalition Against Domestic Violence, boys who witness their fathers battering their mothers are three times more likely as adults to hit their own wives. And sons of the most violent fathers have a rate of wife beating one thousand times greater than do sons of nonviolent fathers.

"Children who grow up in violent homes have a tremendous amount of anger inside that gets transmitted to another generation," says Dee Shepherd-Look, a family violence specialist at California State University at Northridge. "They also learn that violence can be used to control people or situations."

Women who witnessed abuse during their childhood are also at greater risk of experiencing abuse as adults. They come to see violence as an accepted part of a male-female relationship, and tend to get involved with men who abuse women.

The legacy of violence

But it is not just relationships between men and women that are affected by the violence in their partners' past. Continuing the cycle, according to the Center for Health Communication at Harvard School of Public Health, approximately 30 percent of abused children grow up to be abusive parents.

Children who grow up in violent homes learn unhealthy ways of resolving conflict and are at a high risk of becoming abusers themselves.

More than 3 million children witness acts of domestic violence every year. Because children are impressionable, they imitate and repeat what is familiar to them. Children from violent homes are human time bombs set to explode when they become parents or intimate partners, says author Maria Roy. Where there is little family warmth—like hugging and verbal messages of love and caring—and a high level of stress that comes from being afraid of abuse, children do not learn to interact in a gentle, caring way with others. Children raised in violent homes may never have positive role models. They may never have the chance to see effective ways of dealing with stress, anger, or disagreements.

Bordan explains that when violence exists within a family, the family is classified as dysfunctional or troubled.

> In dysfunctional families, children are taught rules of survival: don't talk, don't feel, and don't trust. When they grow up in such a situation, they lack appropriate role models to teach them how to communicate their feelings. They never learn to see what someone who hasn't been abused will see, that the abuse is unnatural.

However, not all members of abusive families grow up to be violent. Of several siblings living in the same environment, only one might grow up to be abusive. When there is a high level of violence in the home, however, chances are that at least one sibling will become an abusing marital partner or parent. Why one and not another? Perhaps one sibling witnessed more abuse longer, received harsher abuse, was the oldest, or was the only male.

There is no guarantee that having witnessed violence as a child will make a person grow up to either accept abuse or to be abusive. There are many women, familiar with the signs of abuse because they saw their mothers being beaten, who

..ABUSE BEGETS ABUSE...

leave their spouse at the first sign of abuse. There are many adults who were abused as children who would never dream of doing the same thing to their own children. And there are many men who witnessed their fathers' abuse of their mothers who have made it a point to avoid such behavior toward their own wives or girlfriends. Many adults emerge determined that no such pattern will repeat itself in them.

In the September/October 1994 issue of *Ms.,* author Rosemary Bray, who grew up with an abusive father, says about her son, Allen:

> I never want to see in Allen's eyes the fearful look that was so often in mine. I never want him to think that hitting people is a good idea, except in

A runaway teenager sits pensively on a city bench. Research has found that troubled teenagers were often abused as children.

circumstances that require him to protect himself. I want with all my heart to stop this cycle, to let it end with me.

Increasingly, researchers and lawmakers are saying that the cycle of violence affects not just one family but society at large by creating a violent atmosphere and increasing criminal behavior among young people. According to the American Psychological Association, children who grow up in violent homes have a 74 percent higher likelihood of committing criminal assaults. Violent juvenile delinquents are four times more likely than are nonviolent juveniles to come from homes in which their fathers beat their mothers.

According to an August 21, 1994, *Chicago Tribune* article, research sponsored by the Justice Department's National Institute of Justice found that abused children are 53 percent more likely to be arrested as juveniles and 38 percent more likely to be arrested as adults. And those who are abused as children are 38 percent more likely to commit a violent crime.

James Garbarino, former president of Chicago's Erikson Institute, a child development research center, asserts that inside particularly troubled teenagers can be found abused children. In the *Chicago Tribune* article, he says:

> If you take almost any major social problem in America and treat it like those Russian nesting dolls, what you will get to is that child abuse would be the last doll—because it is such a profound wound in developing children.

Researchers say that because of the long-lasting damage of family violence, there may be no more costly crime than child abuse.

Opposition to the cycle theory

Not everyone supports the cycle of violence theory as a significant cause of family violence. Some psychologists and researchers warn against relying on the theory to explain why all violence occurs. Sharon Herzberger told the author that while there has been substantial research to suggest the theory puts people at risk for abusive behavior, the percentage of people affected is actually quite small. The best available evidence suggests that approximately one-third of those who were abused become abusers themselves. This means that two-thirds do not. Of those who abuse, estimates of the number who were themselves abused as children range from 18 to 70 percent.

Herzberger explains that just because abusers repeat violence they observed as children does not mean that they were taught to be violent. In other words, Herzberger argues, "the theory is greatly exaggerated. The risk for becoming an abuser is no greater than any of the other reasons cited."

Those who disagree with the intergenerational theory of violence say that the similarities between the abusive parent and child could be based on behaviors their culture feels is acceptable. For example, some cultures believe that a man is the rightful head of his household, who may legitimately use physical force to keep his family in line if necessary. Another theory is that children may inherit their parents' aggressive tendencies genetically.

Herzberger says the cause of abuse might even be a family's social isolation. She explains that sometimes when people start abusing a child or a spouse, they stop socializing with others. "They start limiting their social connections so no one can find out what they are doing," she said. "The more isolated they are, the more likely they are to feel stress, which can cause them to abuse more." But she added that social isolation is not a widely accepted theory for why abuse occurs.

Violence is not inescapable

The danger of relying so heavily on the cycle of violence theory is that people who experience abuse are fearful of what they will be like as parents and spouses. "One person I spoke with said she felt like a closet abuser, though she didn't abuse," Herzberger says. "She was so afraid that one day she would do it because she was fated to do it."

But Shepherd-Look stresses that people do not need to fear that they will be abusive parents or spouses. They can become aware of what could trigger their violent reactions and learn how to handle each situation through parental and marriage counseling.

Another criticism of the intergenerational theory is that it could lead people who did not experience abuse as a child to feel they are not at risk for becoming violent. Norman C. Weissberg, a professor of psychology in New York, says that while there is no doubt that a history of abuse as a child is a risk factor for committing abuse as an adult, the absence of this history does not "immunize one against inflicting harm. . . . The . . . truth is that given the right circumstances we are all 'at risk.'"

The cycle of violence puts everyone—parents, children, spouses, and society—at greater risk of either experiencing abusive situations or of committing them. High risk does not mean that this violence is inescapable. It does mean, however, that people need to be aware of alternative ways of responding to the temptation of violence.

3

In the Child's Best Interest

W HEN CHILD ABUSE is reported—as it is almost 2 million times a year—child protective services must respond. The basic goal of all child protective agencies is to rescue children who are abused or neglected. The system designed to help abused children tries to take their best interests to heart. But knowing what course of action is best for the child is a tough call. Almost every solution—from leaving a child with potentially violent parents, who undergo counseling, to putting a child in foster care—has both benefits and pitfalls.

How agencies should respond and what methods they should use to help the abused child are the subject of much debate within society. Some charge that child protective services, also known as CPS, does too little too late. Others claim there is very little that can be done no matter when CPS enters the family situation. One certainty is that there is no one solution to the problem of how to help an abused child. Should a child be removed from the person who is hurting him or her and sent to live with another family? Some believe that relying on a "when in doubt, pull them out" policy might pose the least risk to the child, but could also destroy a family that might otherwise have been saved. Should the child be left to live with the abuser on the condition that the abuser gets treatment, accepting the risk that the parent will abuse again? These are decisions that child protective services or CPS workers must make every time they respond to a child abuse report.

The CPS process

CPS agencies exist as part of a department of social services in every state. When a child abuse report comes in—often from teachers, doctors, and police—CPS social workers must determine if it should be investigated. They start by asking questions: Is the person who is believed to be the abuser the child's primary caregiver? Is there evidence that the child has been abused, such as a bruise found on the child's face? Is there a witness to the abuse? Is there reason to believe the child is in danger of further abuse?

Whether or not a report should be investigated is not an easy decision for social workers. Some reports seem clear-cut; a caller has seen a parent beating the child and knows the child was injured. Others are less so. For instance, in Chicago in 1994, a social worker received a call about a family who had just brought their three-day-old into a hospital emergency room. The mother, a suspected drug abuser, said the baby had fallen off the bed while the father said that he had accidentally punched the baby in his sleep. Doctors could find no injuries on the baby. The family had five other children and no history of abuse. Though this would ordinarily be considered too weak a case to report, the social worker who took the call decided the baby was at "substantial risk of harm."

If a case is investigated, the social worker who is assigned to the case must do a risk assessment. The worker visits the home of the child, and while there asks questions of the parents, tries to see the child, and generally evaluates the situation. If the social worker thinks the child is in danger, he or she must provide immediate protection to the child so there is no further harm. Social workers can do this by arranging to have the child removed from the home and placed in emergency foster care. For a child to be removed from the home, only two conditions are sufficient and necessary: first, the child was injured or molested, and second, the parents cannot offer a reasonable explanation for that injury.

Sometimes a social worker finds a home situation dangerous enough to require police assistance. Jean Forman, director of the Coalition on Child Abuse and Neglect in New York, says that more and more often the child is found alone in the home.

If CPS social workers think a child needs to be removed from his or her home, either on a

Standing before a judge, a social worker in juvenile/family court argues to have a child removed from an abusive home. The judge will decide if the child is to remain with her parents or be placed in foster care.

temporary or permanent basis, they must go to court within twenty-four to forty-eight hours to petition a judge to make the decision that the child should be removed from the home. There are two courts in which a decision can be made about how to intervene for an abused child. The case can go either to juvenile/family court or criminal court. In family court, a judge can order a child removed from the home if enough evidence exists to make it likely that the child has been abused. In criminal court, the evidence of abuse must be stronger or more definite.

When the judge has heard enough evidence that he or she concludes the child has been abused and is believed to be in danger of further abuse, a decision must be made about the child's welfare. There are three options open to the judge. First, if the judge determines that the family could benefit from home-based counseling, the child will be allowed to stay with the abusive parent. But in this case, the family must go

A couple holds a photo of one of their children who was removed from their home after they were suspected of child abuse. Some question the wisdom of separating a child from his or her parents and prefer instead to keep the family together whenever possible through family preservation programs.

through intensive at-home treatment. Second, the judge may decide that the child should be placed with another family member, such as a grandparent. In more extreme cases, the child may also be placed in foster care, and if parental rights to the child are terminated, even placed for adoption.

Family preservation

The preferred response of child protective services over the last decade has been to keep families together whenever possible through family preservation programs. Forman explains this is because no matter how badly a parent treats a child, if given the choice, a child will usually want to stay with his or her parent. This is not true all of the time, of course. Some children are so badly mistreated that they are relieved to leave their parents.

Family preservation has strong support among those who work in child protective services. They believe that the foster care system is overburdened and the financial cost of placing children in foster care is too high. Out-of-home placements, whether with foster families or relatives, can give a young person badly needed stability if successful. But if unsuccessful, these placements can add to the trauma an abused young person has already suffered. Separation from one's own family, even an abusive family, can also be difficult for a vulnerable young person.

In family preservation programs social workers make frequent visits to the homes of troubled families. Their role is to offer help and advice and to ensure that the child is safe. These visits are aimed at decreasing the stresses that would cause a parent to abuse a child. If financial problems are adding to the stress level in a family, for instance, the social worker might help the family obtain financial aid.

An example of such a program is the Home-builders program, which was developed in Tacoma, Washington, in 1974. The program utilizes a team of professional social workers, psychologists, and counselors who meet with families in their own homes, hear the families define their problems, and stay with them for hours or days at a time for up to six weeks. No team member is responsible for more than three families at one time, allowing for concentrated effort in which to teach the family new ways of coping with their stresses so they will not fall back into their abusive patterns.

A successful program

In the first six years of Homebuilders, placement in foster care became unnecessary for 92 percent of the client families. Without this program as many as 849 children might have been put in foster care or other out-of-home placements. The reason the program is so successful, founders feel, is that it reaches participants before they find themselves at the crisis point of losing their children to foster care or other out-of-home placements. Homebuilders staff are also able to spend more than one hundred hours with each family.

By mid-1987, at least eight states were experimenting with an intensive family services program of this type. Since then, Oregon, Florida, Iowa, Colorado, and Maine have established programs similar to the one in Washington.

Studies indicate that home-based programs have been successful, though long-term benefits have not been researched. Patricia Ryan, the director of the National Family Crisis Resource Center in Michigan, told the author that these programs work well for families in which the abuse is caused by a crisis situation that can be relieved such as the temporary loss of a job or a child care crisis.

However, Ryan says that the decision to use family preservation rather than removing a child from an abusive parent's care must be weighed very carefully. A family's problems may go beyond the issue identified by CPS. Miscalculations by caseworkers have allowed many children to be hurt and sometimes killed by their parents even as the family was undergoing treatment. Ryan says that family preservation does not work well for chronic or long-term abusers, for example. For families in which mental illness is determined to be the cause of child abuse, it would also be dangerous to leave the child in the home.

Foster care

When the abuses cannot be corrected with home-based programs, the child must be removed for his or her own safety. The child can be taken out of the family for a short time while parents undergo counseling. If counseling appears to be successful, the family may eventually reunite. Or the child can be permanently removed from the family and placed for adoption. In either case, the child will probably be placed first in foster care.

The decision to remove a child from his or her home is a drastic step that is usually undertaken only when the child is believed to be in danger of continued abuse. Before a child can be removed from his or her home, the state must prove that the child was abused, with supporting medical reports, for instance. It must also show that the danger of continued abuse persists, perhaps through a parent's threat to further harm the child.

The number of children placed in foster care during the past decade has increased dramatically. In 1990, the U.S. House of Representatives Select Committee on Children, Youth, and Families

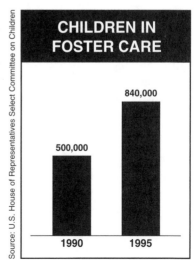

Source: U.S. House of Representatives Select Committee on Children

CHILDREN IN FOSTER CARE

840,000

500,000

1990   1995

estimated that nearly 500,000 children were in out-of-home placement and that by 1995 this number would be more than 840,000 children.

Kinship care

When a child is removed from his or her home, social workers try to find a home in which the child can stay for an extended period if needed. Sometimes the child is sent to a relative who agrees to provide care until other arrangements can be made. Some children placed in foster care, particularly in urban areas, live with relatives who can receive foster care support payments of about $10 a day in a procedure known as "kinship care," which is legal guardianship of a relative.

Because abusive behavior often runs in families, this type of arrangement could replace one abusive household setting with another. For this reason, some social workers hesitate to place a child with a relative. In one Michigan case, for instance, a twelve-year-old girl who was being abused by her stepfather was temporarily placed with her maternal grandparents. The girl's mother protested this arrangement, pointing out that she had been abused by her father and that her daughter might endure similar treatment. If, however, the parent's abusive behavior stems from drug dependency or some other problem that has nothing to do with the family, a loving grandparent or other relative might be just the person to provide much-needed stability in the child's life.

Arrangements such as these always need supervision. Relatives may feel guilty about keeping the parent away from his or her own child and let the abuser into their home for visits. Because their ability to protect the child might be limited this could expose the child to further harm.

When no relative comes forward, unrelated people who are licensed to become foster parents

Foster parents provide safe homes for abused children until their family is able to take them back again or until they can be adopted. Here, a foster parent reads to two first graders.

will take in a child. In Chicago, for example, 90 percent of the 37,000 children in the CPS caseload spend time in one of the city's 10,218 foster homes. Children who are considered difficult—they may be emotionally scarred from the abuse—may be placed with foster parents trained to work intensively with them in what is known as therapeutic foster care. In some foster homes, children may come and go, sometimes daily, sometimes every few months. Caregivers receive about $200 a month to cover the child's expenses, like food and clothing.

A caring environment

When a child is placed in foster care, social workers continue to visit the child's birth home to work on problems so that the family can be reunited. If family preservation programs fail, a parent's rights to the child can be terminated. Then foster care becomes a transition to adoption.

Foster care can be beneficial to children who cannot be with their own parents. Foster homes can provide an abused child with a stable, caring environment until his or her family is able to take the child back again, or until the child can be adopted. Some foster families enter the program specifically because they want to be considered as adoptive parents.

Studies of adults who grew up in foster homes found no evidence that problems such as delinquency, criminality, mental illness, and marital failure occurred more often than in the general population. Other studies found that children who had been in foster care at least a year were rated by their social workers as being better off physically and socially than at the time they entered foster care, and that the well-being of the majority of the children had improved in terms of

physical development, IQ, and school perfor-
mance after six months in foster care.

Hurting instead of helping

But foster care has its drawbacks. For one
thing, it is fairly easy for a family to become licensed as a foster family. As a result, foster families are not carefully screened and some children
wind up being abused in foster homes as well. In
1994, 207 children under the care of Chicago's
child protective services were abused or neglected in foster care either by their foster parents, other adults, or other children. About half of
the 199,000 children who entered foster care nationwide in 1988 were abused or neglected. Many
foster parents want to help children, but some end
up abusing a child because they don't know any
other way to handle the child. "They end up hurting instead of helping," says Ryan.

Foster care programs have also been criticized
for moving children around frequently. Research
has indicated that the majority of children who
remain in foster care for at least six months experience two or more placements. Every time a
child is moved to another home, that child loses a
sense of trust and self-worth. But the real problem comes with the neediest children, who can be
bounced from home to home for years because
their behavior makes it difficult for one family to
keep them for any length of time.

Possibly the biggest problem with the foster
care system is that social workers have very high
caseloads. In some states social workers handle
about fifty cases at any one time, at least forty
more than the Child Welfare League recom-
mends. There are twenty working days in a
month in which social workers must supervise
families, care for them, work with the birth family and foster family, do paperwork, and make

court appearances. If a caseload is only twenty children, that breaks down to about eight hours per month per child, hardly enough to turn most abusive families around. Further, the large caseloads and exhaustive requirements of the job drive many social workers out of the profession after a relatively short time. Those who take their places often receive little training before they begin working with troubled families. "The turnover rate is as high as 70 percent a year," Ryan says, "and they are always running to catch up."

Jumping in the river

While many states are working to improve their child protective services, most social workers agree that the current CPS process is more crisis oriented than preventative. "We intervene okay," says New York's Terry Bordan, "but even then not always successfully. What are we doing to prevent the abuse in the first place?"

There is an analogy social workers use that illustrates this problem well. The story goes that one day a group of social workers stood in a river pulling out drowning baby after drowning baby. They were so busy pulling them out, and still they kept on coming. Finally one social worker said, "This isn't working. What we need to do is go to the head of the river and find out why these babies are being thrown in the water in the first place."

In recent years, child welfare departments nationwide have been criticized for not doing enough to prevent child abuse. They have also been reproached for not doing enough to help children who have been abused. In 1994, the National Committee to Prevent Child Abuse found that CPS social workers did not provide any service in almost 60 percent of confirmed cases of abuse. A review of New York cases, for example, found that almost 56 percent of all confirmed cases were closed the same day the abuse was proven, indicating that little or no action was taken. Nationwide, approximately 290,000 abused children whose cases were reported to CPS in 1994 received no services.

Court-ordered reforms

As a result of complaints like these, more than twenty states are currently undergoing court-ordered reforms of their child welfare departments. Of these, Alabama has made the most progress. While most states are overloaded with children entering state custody, Alabama is among the few actually reducing caseloads. Since 1993, the number of children in state care there dropped 18 percent, largely because of family preservation programs. Training of caseworkers seems to be the key. In Alabama, every social worker's training includes extensive exercises, including role playing to learn how to handle real-life problems.

"Instead of trying to put out the fire, we are trying to see what caused the person to strike the match," says Bonnie Kyles, a social worker from Monroeville, Alabama, in a March 11, 1994, *Chicago Tribune* article. "In the past it was always, 'These are bad people, and these children don't need to be here.' Now we look at strengths and try to build on those strengths."

But any overhaul of the system that is designed to help abused children will not change conditions for the children overnight. It will take many years of trial-and-error changes. In the meantime, though the system fails many children, many abused children do get help.

4

Battered Women and the Justice System

THE JUSTICE SYSTEM—lawmakers, law enforcement, and the courts—has tried to establish ways of dealing with spouse abuse. New laws have made it easier to safeguard victims. But the reality is that the system can only do so much. Sometimes it succeeds in protecting a victim, but sometimes nothing can be done to stop a person intent on abuse—or worse.

"There is no way the legal system can protect a woman whose husband is going to kill her, even with a good system," says family violence specialist Dee Shepherd-Look. "The key is to find ways to help women protect themselves and to make abusers accountable for their actions."

Because spouse beating is a criminal offense in every state, abusers can be held accountable. Depending on the degree of violence, the injuries suffered, and whether any weapons were involved, it is a crime punishable by fines, court-ordered counseling, and/or jail time. The severity of the crime and the penalties differ from state to state. In general, spouse abuse is treated as a misdemeanor when a person causes another injury by

(Opposite page) A woman seeks the court's protection by asking for a restraining order against her husband. Although the justice system tries to protect victims from batterers, it is not always successful in stopping a person intent on abuse.

shoving, pushing, or harassment. A felony, a category of crime more serious in the eyes of the law, occurs when a person threatens another with a weapon or causes damaging physical injuries like head wounds.

Police response

Although the laws treat spouse beating as a crime, police have not always approached domestic abuse as they would other crimes. Police departments receive at least twenty-one thousand spouse abuse calls a week. These were once treated as low priority calls, with many officers reluctant to respond at all. When officers did respond, they rarely made arrests. According to Chief Raymond L. Crawford in Suffolk County, New York:

> Officers had previously been formally trained in academies and informally on the street that you don't get involved in domestic disputes. Your job is to go there and separate them, frighten them, do whatever you have to do, but don't arrest them.

Police officers respond to a domestic violence call. Until recently, police did not always give such calls a high priority.

Even when responding officers felt arrest was called for, they often had difficulty making an arrest stick. Sometimes one or both spouses told police that they had already resolved their problem by the time police arrived. Without the presence of a weapon or a formal complaint by the abused spouse, police could do little. Often a battered woman was too frightened of her husband's threats to press charges or the reality of his being taken away in handcuffs made her change her mind. Sometimes, also, abused spouses called police just to frighten the abuser, never intending to follow through on a complaint. In cases in which the woman did press charges, she might be threatened by the abuser that she was "going to get it later" if she did not drop the charges. In many cases, she did as she was told.

Mandatory arrest policies

Changes in the laws and in police training have given law enforcement agencies new tools for responding to domestic violence. In 1985, many police departments were given the power to arrest even if a victim does not file charges against an abuser. This policy is called the mandatory arrest policy. Also known as the pro-arrest policy, it requires arrests regardless of whether or not an abused partner is willing to press charges. Mandated arrest can occur for felonies and for misdemeanors.

Forty-seven states (excluding Delaware, Vermont, and West Virginia) and the District of Columbia allow police arrest in domestic violence cases even when the victim does not file charges. However, legislation varies from state to state. In Missouri, for example, officers are only mandated to arrest when they are called back to a violent scene within twelve hours. In Hawaii, a police officer may order a suspected batterer to leave the property for a "cooling off" period of twenty-four hours when the officer believes that physical abuse or harm is likely to be inflicted on a family member. If the batterer fails to comply, he can then be arrested.

Mandatory arrest policies appear to have had the added effect of discouraging some would-be abusers. The threat of arrest and the embarrassment of being locked in jail have cut down on some abusive behavior.

Another important benefit of mandatory arrest policies is that they serve as a message to the battered woman that the legal system does not blame her for the abuse and that she does not have to tolerate it. And it gives a strong message to the batterer that his behavior is illegal and he is responsible for it.

But mandatory arrest is not a long-term solution to domestic violence. It is a quick way to calm an explosive situation and to get the abused out of harm's way. The tragic reality is that it is a reactive measure. Before it can be enforced, the victim has to be hurt.

Orders of protection

In recent years, lawmakers have recognized that victims of abuse also need ways to protect themselves before further abuse can occur. One way is the legal instrument called the order of protection or restraining order. Protective orders are court orders that prohibit an accused abuser from entering a residence where the victim lives or from coming within a specified distance of the abused partner. Used in conjunction with the mandatory arrest policy, officers can arrest for violations of an order, punishable by a fine or sentence. Most states give a maximum of six months' jail time and $1,000 in fines for violations.

Protection orders are the most widely used remedy for battering. Every month more than fifty thousand women in the United States seek orders of protection. They are available in all fifty states, as well as the District of Columbia and Puerto Rico. Many battered women prefer getting an order of protection to having their spouse arrested. They hope it will act as a warning to him to stop abusing them.

Most states define the person who is eligible for a protective order as anyone who has an intimate relationship with the abuser. This could include not only the spouse, but children and other relatives who may have been threatened by the abuser as well. States such as Louisiana and Texas even protect foster parents and foster children. A victim could get an order of protection for such actions as threatened injury to herself or her children, destruction of her property, or causing emotional distress. In Illinois, emotional distress includes creating a disturbance at the victim's job, repeatedly phoning her home or office, following her, threatening to take a child, or threatening to enter the victim's residence by force.

Until 1994, a protective order in one state was not always recognized in another. In September 1994 Congress passed the Violence Against Women Act, which established a system for enforcing protection orders in any state. This means that if a woman moves to another state and the abuser follows her there he can be arrested.

Security for the victim

In theory, an order of protection is a good tool; many times it has the desired effect of keeping a victim safe from an abuser. In cases in which an abuser has never been arrested for being violent, chances are he will more likely be deterred from

Lawmakers have realized that victims of abuse need measures to protect themselves against further abuse. Restraining orders were implemented to serve this purpose.

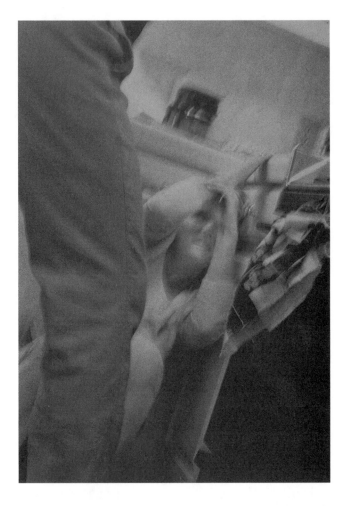

continuing the abuse than someone who has already been arrested for committing a felony. Vicki Lutz, associate director of Battered Women's Justice Center at Pace University in New York, explained to the author that the person who has not run afoul of the justice system has respect for law and order. "He is engaged in anti-social behavior with his partner, but he is more likely to follow the requirements of the order of protection," she says.

Protective orders have other useful benefits as well. They provide security for the victim. They put the police on notice that they need to respond quickly to her calls. And they keep the abuser's name on the court records.

But the protective order does not always do what it is supposed to do. Lutz says that protective orders do more harm than good if courts think of them as a security blanket. She explains:

> Sometimes they might think they don't need to deal with the couple anymore once they issue that order. In the case of a continued aggressor, courts would be better off prosecuting him and putting him in jail and not relying on a piece of paper to stop him from abusing. There is a danger in perceiving orders of protection as a quick fix to domestic violence.

Furthermore, as with mandated arrest, every state has a different version of the policy. In Colorado the police must arrest an abuser who violates a protection order, while in West Virginia, an officer can only make an arrest when he or she sees a violation occurring. This could potentially be a dangerous situation for the woman since it is not likely that an officer would be there in time to protect her from harm.

A license to kill

Another problem is that in most states, restraining orders cannot be mailed and must be served in person to the abuser. Some states authorize a police officer or sheriff to serve an order, but most of the time a victim has to hand an order to the abuser, perhaps provoking anger and an abusive response immediately.

Some broad orders are very strict, like those in New Jersey, which prohibit an abuser from approaching within several feet of the property in which he resides, whether or not he owns it. But sometimes it is the content of the order that creates problems. One New York judge issued a narrowly worded order that restricted the abuser only from entering the couple's bedroom, leaving the woman vulnerable to abusive behavior elsewhere in the house. In other states, judges have been known to divide a house down the middle, another solution that offers only limited protection.

But one of the biggest weaknesses of orders of protection is that no piece of paper can stop the abuser from threatening, harassing, or attacking a person if that is what the abuser wants to do. Despite all of the new laws created to protect victims from abuse, the very pieces of paper designed to protect women—arrest warrants and orders of protection—are sometimes read by enraged men as a license to kill.

An example in Pennsylvania

"A restraining order is a way of getting killed faster," says Park Dietz, a forensic psychiatrist who is a leading expert on homicide. "Someone who is truly dangerous will take this as an extreme denial of what he is entitled to, his God-given right." Acting out that rage, men have been

Members of a Massachusetts community express their outrage over violence against women. As the violence continues, groups throughout the country search for answers to end the abuse.

known to kill not only their partner, but their children, a woman's lawyer, the judge who issued the restraining order, and the officer who made the initial arrest.

Nationwide, the use of orders of protection is constantly being regulated and improved. Pennsylvania offers an example of what states are doing to improve them. The state has a Protection from Abuse Act, a model used in many cities in the United States. The act allows a judge to issue an order of protection based solely on the testimony of the woman, and that order takes effect immediately. Other states require that a witness or the abuser be present, which can cause serious delays at a time when a person may be in danger. In addition, the Pennsylvania law permits other family members to seek a protective order. The order permits the abuser to be evicted from a shared residence, prohibits him from having contact with the abused, grants temporary child custody to the mother, and provides for child support. It further requires the accused to surrender any weapon that may have been used or threatened to be used. If abuse has occurred, it even orders the accused to pay for medical, counseling, and other expenses relating to the attack. Violation of the Pennsylvania law is punishable by up to six months in jail and a $1,000 fine.

Antistalking legislation

There are times when an order of protection does not prevent an abuser from harassing or stalking his victim. Some abusive ex-husbands or former boyfriends have been known to make threatening phone calls or sit outside a woman's residence or job in an effort to threaten her or do further harm.

Since 1990, antistalking legislation has been enacted nationwide. Though it is defined differently

More powerful than orders of protection, antistalking laws carry stiffer penalties. If convicted, a person who violates antistalking laws can be sentenced to five years in prison.

in every state, it is a law aimed at protecting women before they get hurt. Antistalking laws usually allow arrests for harassment. In the past, police were not able to make an arrest unless an order of protection had been violated and the abuser physically assaulted the victim. Now an abuser can be arrested before an order of protection is violated.

Antistalking laws are more powerful than orders of protection. A person who violates antistalking laws can be charged with either a misdemeanor or a felony. A conviction can result in a fine of up to $10,000 and five years in prison. However, most states carry a penalty of one year in jail and a $1,000 fine for first-time offenders. The federal Violence Against Women Act, passed as part of the 1994 anticrime legislation, makes it a crime for a stalker to cross state lines or use the mail or telephone to make threats.

Additionally, antistalking laws can offer battered women a greater sense of security. Mona Lou Callery, who was physically abused by her spouse for several years, told the author that she wishes there had been an antistalking law in place for her. She left her abusive husband in 1985, taking her three children. He terrorized her until her divorce was final five years later, the same year the antistalking legislation passed. Because there was no antistalking law, she could not stop him.

> There wasn't a day that went by that he didn't call me, send someone over with candy for the kids, drive by my house. I thought if I didn't kill him, I would kill myself. I tried to move through the court system, but no one could keep him away from me. The antistalking laws are a great relief to battered women.

The role of the courts

Once an abuser is charged with a crime, whether it is a misdemeanor or a felony, he is brought into a court to be arraigned, a preliminary step to trial and possible punishment if he is found guilty. At this point, the accused enters a plea, and the court sets bail or the abuser is released until his trial date.

It is not always easy to get a spouse abuse case to this stage. Some judges have old-fashioned ideas about how family matters should be handled. Extreme examples of judges' decisions have been collected by the National Clearinghouse for the Defense of Battered Women. One Pennsylvania district court judge, after hearing a wife present her case against her violent husband, leaned over the bench and smiled at the husband and said, "If I were you I would have hit her, too." In another case, a Kansas judge suspended the fine of a convicted abuser and ordered him to go out and buy his wife a box of candy.

Attitudes such as these are not the norm, however. In many states, including New York, California, and Oklahoma, judges are required to take part in domestic violence awareness training.

They are taught the dynamics of abusive relationships so they will have a better understanding of the cases they deal with.

Attorney Meredith Hofford of the National Council of Juvenile and Family Court Judges in Nevada told the author that she finds most judges are "well intentioned, but in the case of family violence, not very well informed. But when they become better informed and understand the dynamics and options, they tend to respond much better to these cases in courts."

Untried and unpunished

But even when judges are open-minded about family violence, many cases are dismissed. Many times courts must deal with victims who will not press charges, who drop the charges, or who suddenly back out and disappear. One assistant district attorney in the Bronx, New York, says that frequently women say things like "He learned his lesson. I don't need to take this further." As a result, many cases of abuse go untried and unpunished. Lutz says women drop nearly 50 percent of all domestic violence charges. They may do this because they have been intimidated into not pressing charges against their abuser. They may have been threatened with a custody battle by the abuser if they carried through on the charges. Or they may be afraid of what a potential loss of income can mean to their children if a spouse has to serve jail time. Many others are in hiding and unavailable for court appearances.

Such reluctance frustrates people in the court system who are trying to help victims of abuse. So some cities have come up with other ways of bringing some of these cases to trial. They have designed a cutting-edge legal policy, victimless prosecution, first used in Duluth, Minnesota, in 1984. It allows a case to be prosecuted without a victim's presence. The case is then based on evidence from 911 tapes, photographs, physical evidence taken from the scene of an assault, medical records, and witness reports.

One interesting aspect of victimless prosecution is that a victim's "excited utterances" are also allowed as evidence. Excited utterances are a victim's conversation heard by police or other witnesses during or shortly after an attack when she might be too upset to speak clearly. In Seattle, where excited utterances are allowed in court, Jennifer Mantz, head of the city's interim domestic violence unit, says, "If the officer describes the victim as so agitated she can hardly speak, then she is considered too upset to have made up a story."

Victimless prosecution has been used successfully in Philadelphia; San Diego; Quincy, Massachusetts; and Tulsa, Oklahoma. For example, of the four to five hundred domestic violence cases San Diego prosecutes a month, almost 60 percent involve victimless prosecution.

More enlightened courts

As more judges and juries become sensitive to why a woman might not want to appear in front of her abuser during a trial, victimless prosecution is becoming an effective way to bring abuse cases to trial. This change suggests that courts are becoming more enlightened about domestic violence. "They are now willing to convict if they hear all the evidence, whether the victim is there or not," says Lutz.

Perhaps the most important aspect of mandatory arrest policies, laws, and other antistalking legislation is that they serve as an important link for battered women to the criminal justice and social service systems. Many battered women first hear about their legal rights and the support their

An accused batterer and his lawyer appear before a judge. Victimless prosecution, which allows a case to be prosecuted without a victim's presence, has become an effective way to encourage victims of abuse to bring their cases to trial.

community offers from the police officers who respond to their call. In recent years, the police have made most of the referrals to domestic violence programs for women, as well as to criminal and protection order courts.

To foster that link, advocates for battered women are designing a community approach to handling domestic violence. In many states, police, courts, hospitals, educators, psychologists, and social workers are working together to help end domestic violence in their communities.

Sara Buel, an attorney in Boston who has herself been battered, says, for example, that the Quincy, Massachusetts, court has been a national leader in protecting battered women with comprehensive assistance and legal action so effective that some abuse survivors move there to feel safe.

A national program

In February 1995, the American Bar Association formed the Commission on Domestic Violence with representatives from the American Medical Association, the National Education Association, the American Psychological Association, the National Resource Center on Domestic Violence, and the military, law enforcement, media, and business communities. Their purpose was to use their combined resources to address the issue of solving domestic violence through community-based programs. The commission plans to create a national program that will give battered women access to all the help they need to lead lives without abuse.

Furthermore, the passage of the Violence Against Women Act makes violence against women a federal crime. It also designates $800 million to restructure the criminal justice system's responses to spouse abuse so that in the future, women can expect more protection from outside of their home.

5

When the Abused
Kill Their Abusers

FAMILY VIOLENCE CAN sometimes become so painful and so overwhelming that the abused believes the only way to stop the attacks is to kill the abuser. This does not happen often. Each year between three and four hundred children commit parricide, or murder of their parents. Of those, 90 percent had been victims of constant and severe abuse, according to Paul Mones, a Los Angeles attorney who specializes in defending adolescents who have killed their abusive parents. An average of five hundred women, the majority of whom have endured years of abuse, kill their husbands and boyfriends each year.

Cases such as these are usually more complex than they at first appear. Often, the abused person contends the killing was an act of self-defense, convinced that was the only action that would protect him or her from further harm. But the circumstances of the killing may not fit the traditional scenario of self-defense. Self-defense is usually seen as an act required to protect oneself from an immediate threat of harm or death. Killings of abusers often take place when no immediate threat exists. Nevertheless, many abuse victims who kill their abusers view their actions

(Opposite page) A woman convicted of killing her abusive husband looks through the barbed wire fences at a Raleigh, North Carolina, prison. Many abuse victims who kill their abusers view their actions as self-defense.

as their only salvation from continuing pain and injury. "The ultimate protection is to kill the aggressor after years of abuse," says Terry Bordan.

The tales of abuse that are heard during trials are often as horrifying as the desperate act of murder itself. The story of eighteen-year-old Robert Moody of California is typical. Moody killed his abusive father with three shotgun blasts in 1989. During the four-day trial, the judge heard evidence that Robert's father had terrorized the family for years. He had encouraged Robert to take drugs and watch pornographic movies, raped two of Robert's sisters, fondled another, and forced Robert's mother to become a prostitute to pay for a boat he wanted. The judge also heard evidence that the shooting took place a few hours after Robert had witnessed his father beating his mother. The judge called Robert's dead father the "scum of the earth." Moody was convicted of murder, but given a four-year suspended prison sentence, with five years of probation and an order to spend two years abroad working as a Christian missionary.

A matter of time

Many factors can drive a person to murder a parent or spouse. Usually the abused has experienced extreme violence over a long period of time. Children, in particular, may have suffered years of sexual abuse as well as physical abuse that began when they were babies. Beatings may have been so severe that the victims thought they were going to die from the injuries. In many cases, the abuser threatened the abused with death at one time or another.

Those who endure severe and ongoing abuse may see their own deaths as not far off. They lose all hope for any possibility of improvement or relief. The abuse is a constant reminder of how powerful the abuser is and how he or she can act without fear of being stopped. Victims may come to believe that they are powerless to stop the abuse or even their approaching death.

Louise Bill, chairperson of the department of public administration and human services at Kennesaw State College in Georgia, explains that "People who murder their abusers after enduring abuse over a long period of time see no other way out. It is almost a rational decision, a dramatic attempt at self-preservation."

Victims who kill their abusers act out of a feeling that they are trapped and that there is no other choice to be made. Women may have tried to move through the criminal justice system and found that an order of protection did not stop the abuser from continuing attacks. "It might have angered him so that he beat her up more," says Bill. The woman may have isolated herself from help because of embarrassment and decided she had no choice but to help herself. Or she may have been told by the abuser that if she tried to get help or leave him, he would find her and kill her. Another typical threat involves children. The

Meekah Scott, who was convicted of murdering her batterer and served time in prison, attends a rally against domestic violence, hoping to help end the type of abuse that drove her to kill.

abuser may threaten to take the children away from her. If she tries to leave or even get a job, he may threaten to get her fired. "These batterers usually carry through on their threats. The woman is controlled when she stays and threatened when she leaves," says Bill.

An act of hopelessness

For young people who have been abused, there are even fewer alternatives. It is against the law for them to run away from home. They may not know where or how to get help. Because of their age, young people may not have the ability to weigh alternatives to killing their abusers.

Life becomes increasingly intolerable for the abused; eventually, they see no other way out of the violence than to kill their abuser. Bill explains: "If they live like this year after year, it's not surprising that they kill their abusers. I am surprised there aren't more murders. The act of murder itself becomes an act of hopelessness."

While many people are abused and never reach the point at which they would kill their abusers, some are pushed one step too far. What triggers the killing is usually either a real or imagined difference in the abuser's behavior. Typically, the victim sees the situation as more threatening than usual. The abuser may be drinking or taking drugs more frequently. The violence may be more frequent and extreme. Whichever the case the victim believes the behavior is out of control and that it can lead to death at any moment.

In November 1982, for instance, sixteen-year-old Richard Jahnke and his seventeen-year-old sister, Deborah, after many years of being beaten and tortured by their father, ambushed and killed him outside of their Cheyenne, Wyoming, home. They planned the attack after their father warned

Richard that he had better not be home when the father got back from an outing. This was a threat Richard had never heard from his father before and he believed he had no choice but to take action that would save his own life. Likewise, in 1989, fifteen-year-old Diana Goodykoontz of Pensacola, Florida, murdered her father by shooting him in the chest with his own gun after he threatened to kill her, her mother, and two siblings.

A defense for murder

Together, these are the kinds of circumstances that can turn an abuse victim into a killer. Once cases such as these move through the court system the question of guilt rarely is at issue. Usually the battered person does not try to cover up the crime. In most cases, the person not only confesses to the killing, but also is the one to call the police and an ambulance. The killer usually pleads guilty, and depending upon the state, can be given a life sentence or the death penalty. But these sentences are rare. The events that lead to the murder often invite compassion and a lesser sentence for the offender. Most abuse victims who kill their abusers are convicted of manslaughter and receive sentences ranging from one to twenty years, with fifteen years being the average.

Within the last decade, defense attorneys have encouraged victims of abuse to accept a plea of guilty by reason of self-defense, claiming that the murder was an act of protection brought on by years of abuse. This defense, first used in the 1980s, has gained increasing support within the legal community in the last ten years. By using the self-defense theory for the murder, they have the chance to reduce the sentence for a person who has already suffered years of abuse.

A woman demonstrates at the Boston state house in support of eight women serving prison terms in Massachusetts for killing their abusers.

But self-defense is not an easy case to make. Traditionally, a person may lawfully use physical force against another in self-defense only when there is a reasonable belief that the other is threatening him or her with imminent danger or serious bodily harm and that such force is necessary to prevent the harm. Self-defense usually requires that the appearance of danger must have been so real that a reasonable person, faced with the same circumstances, would have done the same thing.

All of these conditions would seem to fit the profile of a battered person driven to murder. But this use of traditional self-defense also requires that persons act to protect themselves during an attack. Typically, however, the abuser is killed while sleeping or through a surprise attack. It is rare that the abused kills the abuser while in the heat of a beating. Because women and children are most often the victims of abuse, and because they are smaller than their abusers, they rely more often on the element of surprise to halt the ongoing attacks. This makes the self-defense claim harder to prove since a sleeping person, for example, does not threaten immediate harm. "Self-defense could be a good defense," says Bill, "if the attacks were not usually done when there was no immediate attack."

An overkill factor

Sometimes abused persons hire someone else to do the killing because they feel they are incapable of doing it themselves. Facing charges of conspiracy to commit murder, self-defense becomes even more questionable. One widely publicized case occurred in Long Island, New York, in 1989. Sixteen-year-old Cheryl Pierson hired a classmate, Sean Pica, to kill her sexually abusive father for $1,000. Pica committed the murder, pleaded guilty to manslaughter, and was sentenced to eight to twenty-four years in prison for killing "out of sheer greed," according to the judge. Pierson was sentenced to six months in jail and five years' probation. She served three and a half months before she was released. Pierson had

Cheryl Pierson, pictured with her boyfriend, paid a classmate $1,000 to kill her abusive father. After proving a history of abuse, she was sentenced to six months in jail and served three and a half months.

been able to prove a history of abuse and show that she had acted out of fear that her sister was going to be abused by their father as well. In addition, her stepbrother and neighbors testified that they had suspected she was being abused, but had done nothing to help her.

Another complication is that murders by young people, in particular, have an overkill factor. "They don't just shoot once, or stab once. They usually riddle a body with wounds," says Mones. To a jury, this casts doubt on the defendant's helplessness and suggests both cruelty on the part of the killer and a more coolly calculating intent.

Expert witnesses

Some states require that defendants show that they tried every avenue to "retreat" from the violence, though sometimes an exception is made when the threat occurs within a person's home. In the case of battered women and children, who may have seen no retreat, they may believe based on their experience that they are in danger of being severely beaten or killed if they do not try to kill the person when they can.

To show that the killer's actions were reasonable, expert witnesses are often asked to explain in court how a history of violence could lead a person to murder an abuser. Usually the battered person syndrome (or battered woman or child syndromes) is introduced as evidence to explain the psychological state of the killer at the time of the murder. This syndrome is similar to posttraumatic stress disorder, a psychological condition common among prisoners of war. People who are repeatedly and unpredictably exposed to attacks by another person develop certain psychological symptoms such as a fear of frequent and unexpected violent attacks and flashbacks that affect their ability to function long after the incident is passed. In other words, the spouse or child experiences a heightened sensitivity to the abuser's behavior and lives in constant fear of the next beating. They can become so terrified that they believe they can do nothing to change the situation except get rid of the abuser. Accepting this as evidence can help convince the court that the killer had reasonable belief, based on past interactions with the abuser, that he or she was in "imminent danger of great bodily harm," at the time of the murder. In the case of Goodykoontz, for example, the judge agreed with expert witnesses that she acted out of fear of harm and that she reasonably believed that the use of deadly force was necessary.

Increased acceptance of self-defense plea

Many judges, however, refuse to allow such a defense in their courts. In a 1988 California case, Brenda Aris shot and killed her husband while he lay unconscious after consuming large quantities of alcohol. She testified she was afraid he would start beating her again when he regained consciousness. The judge allowed testimony describing battered woman syndrome, but not evidence that the syndrome applied in Aris's case. Even though at the time of her arrest her entire body was covered with black-and-blue marks, she was found guilty of second-degree murder. The judge had not informed the jury about the use of the self-defense plea, so she went to jail.

Attorney Sarah Buel of the Massachusetts Council on Domestic Violence explained to the author judges' reactions to the self-defense plea:

A lot of judges won't allow this claim because they are not familiar with the issues. They don't understand the dynamics of battered women and children. When they do, there is a higher likelihood that all relevant evidence will be admitted to the case.

Increasingly the reaction of the judicial system is more compassionate to the killer in abuse cases. As public awareness of these cases increases, arguments by defense attorneys that women and children act in self-defense are becoming more accepted among judges. And legislation in some states, including Massachusetts, directs judges to allow a self-defense claim for anyone—man, woman, or child—who has been battered and then murdered their abuser. Buel, a former battered wife who put herself through Harvard Law School after she left her husband, says:

> We did this so that judges could no longer treat these situations on a case-by-case basis. We wanted every battered person to expect that a judge would understand their situation.

A criticism of the self-defense plea is that it can itself be abused. A sensational example is the 1993 Menendez brothers' trials in California. These trials resulted in hung juries when jurors could not decide if twenty-two-year-old Lyle and eighteen-year-old Erik Menendez, who claimed their parents had sexually abused them, murdered their parents in self-defense. The trials were complicated by the fact that the parents were multimillionaires. Many people agreed with the prosecutors' claims that the brothers made up the history of abuse, exploiting the battered child defense, because they wanted to inherit their parents' money. An imperfect self-defense theory was allowed, which asserts that the defendants believed their lives to be in danger even though a reasonable person in the same circumstances would not see it that way.

Richard Jahnke, charged with second-degree murder, pleaded self-defense in the murder of his

Many people believe that Erik and Lyle Menendez made up a history of abuse to use the battered child defense to escape responsibility for murdering their wealthy parents.

father and was found guilty of first-degree manslaughter. He was sentenced to five to fifteen years in prison, but the governor of Wyoming reduced his sentence to two years in response to public outcry. His sister Deborah had been sentenced to three to eight years; her sentence was reduced to one year of probation.

The complex legal issues in battered women's and children's self-defense cases are varied, often not well understood, and sometimes ambiguous. The use of this defense is fairly new and there is as yet no body of precedents for judges to draw on. But the use of battered person syndrome to support self-defense pleas is an example of what might be done to help women and children who kill their abusers after years of abuse. It does not attempt to explain away or condone what they feel they had been forced to do. Instead, it is a way to suggest how justice can still be applied to cases in which justice was tragically missing. When battered persons believe they are defending their lives in committing murder, justice is not always clear.

Ending Family Violence

EFFORTS TO END family violence have combined many ideas and approaches. But the concept that domestic violence can be prevented is new to those who work with troubled families. For the last twenty years, the approach to the issue has been mostly reactive. When a spouse is battered, the criminal justice system moves in to try to protect her. When a child is abused, social workers attempt to stop further abuse. But this protection is not available until after a person has been hurt.

As society has come to realize how widespread the problem of family violence is, people have been moved to develop programs that can prevent the abuse from happening in the first place. Since 1994, there has been a national focus on developing child abuse and spouse abuse prevention efforts.

One philosophy behind programs to prevent child abuse is that if parents learn ways to handle their anger and stress, they will not abuse their children and will most likely not abuse each other. According to Leslie Mitchel, director of Healthy Families America:

> By all accounts, our experiences in the field of child welfare have shown that the crisis-driven,

(Opposite page) At a rally against domestic violence, Midge Obrinske wipes a tear from her eye as she holds a sign in memory of her granddaughter, Mindy Reed, who was killed by her boyfriend. Efforts to end the widespread problem of family violence have begun to focus on prevention.

reactive approach to assisting overburdened families and vulnerable children has failed. To make the difference in the lives of families, we must offer support early—when parents are expecting their first child.

To this end, new and promising programs are appearing in the area of child abuse prevention.

Home visiting programs

In 1994, the U.S. Congress passed the Federal Family Preservation and Support Act, which authorized $1 billion over five years to encourage new approaches to family violence prevention. One of the most popular approaches is home visiting programs, widely considered the most promising effort to prevent child abuse because they bring help directly to the place where most abuse occurs.

The goal of home visiting is to teach families at high risk for violent behavior ways to communicate anger with words rather than with fists. Child welfare agencies, private organizations, and community groups across the country join in targeting primarily pregnant women and parents of newborns. Because infancy and toddlerhood are when children are most vulnerable to child abuse, researchers have found that providing education and support to high-risk households around the time of a baby's birth, and continuing for many months or years afterward, significantly reduces the risk of child abuse. Families who receive intensive home visitor services modeling positive, healthy child-rearing practices also show a decrease in the high-risk factors that may lead to abuse and neglect. For instance, parents who go through the program are more likely to graduate from high school and get jobs, which reduces their chance of financial stress.

Programs that work with new parents stand the greatest chance of success because new parents are often eager and excited to learn about caring for their babies. Home visiting programs model and support positive parenting practices before bad patterns are established.

"Home visiting programs are good because they are reaching families when they are most willing to be reached, with their first baby," Jean Forman, director of the Coalition on Child Abuse and Neglect in New York, told the author. "Parents need support with their first babies, to set the groundwork for the future."

Healthy Families America

A national home visiting program was launched in 1992 by the National Committee to Prevent Child Abuse. Called Healthy Families America, it is based on the Healthy Start program

A mother enrolled in the Healthy Baby program at her hospital undergoes an exam by her obstetrician. Like Healthy Families America, the Healthy Baby program follows mothers through pregnancy, childbirth, and the first year and teaches stress reduction and positive parenting skills.

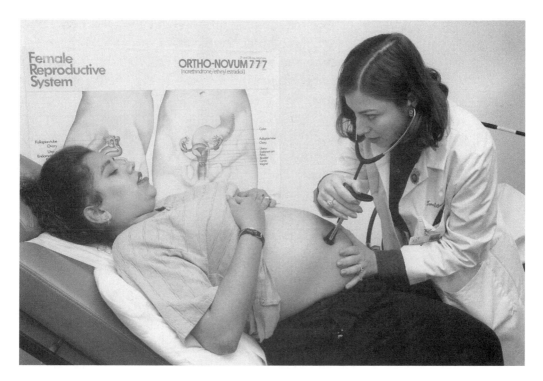

created in Hawaii in July 1985. Healthy Start began as a three-year demonstration program for high-risk families in Leeward, Oahu, a multiethnic, poor area with high unemployment and substandard housing. Three years into the program, not one case of child abuse had been reported among the 241 families in the program. During this same period, abuse was reported in families that did not take part in the program. The program was expanded, and by July 1993, Healthy Start was reaching 51 percent of Hawaii's families with newborns.

Healthy Families America, like its prototype, is designed to improve family coping skills and to promote positive parenting practices and parent-child interaction. Its work usually begins when a woman enters a hospital to have her baby. At that time, caseworkers interview her, using a family stress checklist of risk indicators. Questions include whether or not the mother is married, if her income is adequate to cover living expenses, if she has a home for the child, a high school education, and a history of substance abuse. If the family is determined to be at high risk for abuse, members are encouraged to accept home visiting services. The services are optional, so if a mother decides she is not interested, she does not have to go through the program. But researchers have found that the majority of women agree to participate. During the three-year demonstration period in Hawaii, 95 percent of the families contacted accepted the services.

Emotional support

During hospital and home visits, caseworkers help participants sort out a variety of problems ranging from finding better housing to obtaining food when it is in short supply. They also teach the woman how to care for her baby. They focus primarily on providing emotional support to parents and showing useful skills in dealing with everyday problems. They also teach parents how to interact with their child, working on such things as how to make sure the baby eats properly.

The program is intensive. All families receive weekly visits when they first enter the program. When they demonstrate that they are handling stressful situations well and that they interact well with their children, they can graduate to quarterly visits. These can continue until the child is five years old, when the child typically enters school and families can qualify for other support services.

While most of the program is aimed at the mother, fathers are asked to participate, as well. Sometimes male home visitors work with fathers to make sure they participate in raising their child. Mitchel says that where working with males has been a priority, male visitors have been able to teach men ways to stop themselves from becoming abusive of spouses and have helped them to get jobs.

Opening the door

One home visitor said of the program, "Many families just need to be nurtured themselves before they can nurture their children. It is like opening a door for them just as they opened a door for me."

Today there are more than twelve hundred Healthy Families America programs in twenty-two states. Planning is under way to include the program as part of all states' long-term strategies for supporting families. Most other states have established task forces to explore the development of these efforts. The Healthy Families America program also incorporates and builds on other existing community programs, such as hot-

Holding her four-month-old baby, a teenage parent learns coping skills in a program designed to help lessen the stress of parenthood.

lines people can call when they feel they need help.

Home visiting is considered to be a cost-effective way to deal with child abuse. Genevieve Migely, a research analyst at the National Committee to Prevent Child Abuse, told the author that intensive home visits to a single family cost about $2,500 a year. A nationwide program would cost one-third to one-half of the estimated $9 billion spent annually on treating child abuse. In other words, she says, for every $3 spent on prevention, at least $6 is saved that might have been spent on child welfare services, foster care, or counseling. It is cheaper to keep children out of the child welfare system than to treat them after they have been abused.

Teaching kids how to resolve conflict without violence

While parents are the target for prevention of abuse with young children, programs are also being aimed at school-aged children. Young people are being taught by teachers and visiting social workers methods to communicate and to handle their anger with choices other than using violence. They are learning these skills in school.

Dee Shepherd-Look told the author:

> The biggest trend has been to move into the schools—elementary, junior high, and high school. There you can teach verbal and conflict-resolution skills while kids are still impressionable. We know from all the studies done on the most violent people, that one of the overriding characteristics is that the abuser does not know how to communicate. If you don't have skills to deal with conflict, you can wind up pummeling someone.

While some educators feel it is not their job to be social workers, many have found that what goes on in a child's home affects what happens in the classroom. Lydia Axelrod, a New York school superintendent, says: "The educational process is often impeded by the condition youngsters are in when they come to school. We can no longer look the other way."

Strengthening self-esteem

Various projects around the country use trained local volunteers to conduct ongoing, hour-long workshops in schools. Using role-playing techniques, children learn how to protect themselves, how to avoid abusive situations, and how to exercise their rights. Most importantly, according to Forman, the sessions strengthen a child's self-esteem. In effect, she explains, these programs are preventative. If children learn at a young age how to communicate their anger, they will be less likely to abuse their children and spouses in the future.

"These programs give kids the words to say 'no' to being abused by their parents or anyone, for instance," says Forman. "They also learn what is acceptable behavior and what is wrong. By

As part of the Resolving Conflict Creatively Program at a public school in New York City, students develop their conflict-resolution skills.

confronting the issue of family violence, children are being educated for the future."

One of the most widely used programs is the Resolving Conflict Creatively Program (RCCP), an initiative of Educators for Social Responsibility. It began in 1985 in New York City public schools, and is now the largest program in the country. In 1995, it served 150,000 children in 325 schools nationwide, including schools in Alaska, Louisiana, California, and New Jersey. This program relies on support from teachers and principals to introduce conflict-resolution skills. These include active listening, expressing feelings, cooperation, negotiation, and communication.

Linda Lantieri, director of the RCCP, explains:

> We have found that, in these times, to be an educated person requires not only the traditional reading, writing, and mathematical skills, but also the

skills to deal with feelings appropriately, to communicate clearly, and to resolve conflicts nonviolently.

A three-year study of the effectiveness of RCCP began in 1993. It is funded by the U.S. Centers for Disease Control and Prevention. But an independent analysis by Metis Associates in 1990 found that 87 percent of all teachers who used the program said that it had a positive impact in helping students to deal with violence and violence-related behavior. The study concluded that children had increased self-esteem and a sense of empowerment, as well as an increased awareness of their feelings and how to verbalize those feelings.

Re-education about male-female relationships

In addition to school-based programs like the Resolving Conflict Creatively Program, many community groups offer to speak to students about violence. Joan Sculli, executive director of the Nassau County Coalition Against Domestic Violence, Inc., in New York, frequently speaks to teenagers in schools about domestic violence. She says that adolescence is an important time to educate children about violence. They are beginning to develop male-female relationships, and can easily copy dysfunctional family situations. She says she tells students, "If you are a girl and your boyfriend slaps you, even if he says he is only kidding, ask him to get help and then leave the relationship." She tells students that once someone feels it is okay to hit a female, he is not likely to stop later on. And she tells boys that if they find themselves wanting to hit their girlfriends or have already done so, talk to the school counselor.

Peer support groups like Natural Helpers are also used in many junior high and high schools throughout the country to offer young people outlets to communicate their problems. Natural Helpers was founded in Seattle in 1979 by the Comprehensive Health Education Foundation. The program is based on the idea that each school has an informal helping network of students and teachers whom students trust with their problems and concerns. The program trains these students and adults as Natural Helpers so they can better help those young people who come to them. Natural Helpers are also taught how to use their school and community services and how to refer the student in need.

"There's no excuse"

Family violence awareness programs are another method of prevention. The goal of this approach is to show witnesses to abuse how to respond. A poll taken by the Family Violence Prevention Fund in 1993 found that 34 percent of all adults in the United States have witnessed domestic violence. The poll also indicated that the majority of Americans recognized that domestic violence is a problem. But when it came to doing something about the problem, they felt helpless to stop it.

In response, the San Francisco–based organization developed the first national public service campaign intended to promote the prevention of domestic violence. The campaign, called "There's No Excuse for Domestic Violence," debuted in June 1994 in television, radio, and print.

The purpose of this program is to encourage understanding about the problem of domestic violence in the hope that people will recognize their own or an acquaintance's improper behavior, as well as encouraging the public to take action if they suspect abuse is happening. They are encouraged to call the police, for instance, if a

Two of the thousands of marchers in a recent march against domestic violence remind the public that family violence is still a major societal problem.

FORTY-TWO PERCENT OF ALL MURDERED WOMEN ARE KILLED BY THE SAME MAN.

Each day women are beaten to death by their husbands or boyfriends. Just as frightening, each day neighbors just like us make excuses for not getting involved. For information about how you can help stop domestic violence, call 1-800-777-1960.

THERE'S **NO** EXCUSE
for Domestic Violence.

Ad Council

Family Violence Prevention Fund

As part of the effort to draw attention to the abuse problem in the United States, the Family Prevention Fund developed a campaign called "There's No Excuse for Domestic Violence." The program encourages the public to take action if they suspect abuse is happening.

neighbor's argument seems to have escalated or if they see a stranger slap another in the street.

In one commercial, a couple are about to go to sleep when a violent fight breaks out between a man and a woman in the apartment above them. The couple listen but, not knowing what to do, they turn off the light. The spot ends with the message, "It is your business."

Program organizers do not yet have statistics on how much the campaign has been able to prevent abuse. But they do believe that the number of reports of domestic violence to the police has increased since the program began.

Model code against spouse abuse

In addition to these public campaigns, a national effort is under way to support legislation to prevent spouse abuse. In 1993, the U.S. Department of Health and Human Services provided funding to establish a network of domestic violence resource centers. Since then, the network has been drafting legislation and working to gather statistics and other information about spouse abuse. Their joint goal is to help improve the legal, medical, and social response to violence against women.

The passage of the Violence Against Women Act in 1994 ensures that there is more money available to meet these goals. It also makes funding ready for a national domestic violence hotline, which is due to open in 1996. A hotline is a number that people can call if they feel they are in danger of abuse or if they need advice on how to handle their violent situation. The previous national hotline was closed due to lack of federal funding in 1993. Since then, individual states have had to fund their own hotline when they could.

Along with these promising changes at the federal level, most states are working on their own to create programs to deal with the issue of family violence. As a guideline, family violence specialists are using the model plan developed by the Family Violence Project of the National Council of Juvenile and Family Court Judges in Nevada. It is the result of a three-year project to analyze state legislation on family violence. According to Meredith Hofford, the director of the project, "Everything that has been done in the issue of do-

Staff from the Child Welfare League of America answer calls from children who are being abused and from those who want to report child abuse. Such hotlines provide callers with advice on what they can do and who they can contact for help.

mestic violence has been piecemeal. Every state is doing something different. Our idea was to research the best of what every state had to offer, and combine them into a model program."

The model code was released in 1994. It provides states with information about things like how to improve methods for using protection orders and criminal procedures with batterers. The program's main objectives for the model code are for states to treat domestic violence as a crime; to provide for the safety and well-being of children; to offer procedures for protection of victims; and to promote community response to family violence.

Hopes for a violence-free generation

Since 1994, Georgia, for instance, has formed a state commission on family violence, which has been charged with developing ways to deal with the issue. Twenty-eight task forces have been formed around the state, and the plan provides for nineteen more. According to Louise Bill, chairperson of the department of public administration and human services at Kennesaw State College in Georgia, already the state has programs to teach batterers better ways to handle their anger than to hit. It has also established shelters for abused women to seek protection from abusers, and made the medical community more aware of how to work with battered family members.

Though public awareness has spurred efforts to enact more legislation and activate more programs to help victims of abuse, experts still search for programs to end the legacy of family violence.

According to Hofford, the ultimate goal of the model code program is to enact unified national legislation about family violence prevention. In the meantime, says Bill, society will have to rely on each individual state's efforts to thwart the family violence that already exists. She concludes:

> Family violence is like the chicken and the egg question. What comes first? Can we really prevent family violence when we are trying to help people who are already being abused? All we can hope for is that when all the programs are in place, eventually they will be fully preventative.

Ultimately, this is what people who work with the issue of family violence are striving for. By providing preventative programs to families identified as high risk for violence today, the next generation of intimate partners and parents may be able to live violence free.

Glossary

antistalking legislation: Laws that make it illegal for a person to willfully, maliciously, and repeatedly follow and harass another person.

battered child syndrome: Similar to battered woman syndrome and used to refer to a child who has a psychological disorder as a result of repeated gross abuse.

battered person syndrome: Similar to battered woman syndrome and used to refer to anyone who has a psychological disorder as a result of repeated abuse.

battered woman syndrome: A psychological disorder that is the result of repeated and unavoidable abuse that usually leaves victims in a constant state of fear of further injury or death.

battering: Intentional physical violence, such as punching, against another person.

caregiver: Anyone who is legally responsible for the care of a child.

child abuse: Any form of physical, emotional, or neglectful mistreatment of a child that results in pain, distress, or endangerment.

child protective services: State organizations established as part of the social welfare system to protect children from further mistreatment by an abuser.

conflict-resolution skills: Communication skills that teach people how to handle stressful situations without resorting to violence.

cycle of violence: A behavioral theory of a pattern of abuse in which children who either are abused or witness abuse grow up to repeat that mistreatment in their own families.

domestic violence: Abuse that occurs between family members.

excited utterances: An abuse victim's conversation overheard by witnesses after a battering incident; can be used as evidence against the abuser in court.

failure to protect: A component of child abuse laws that makes it illegal for a nonabusing parent not to stop child abuse at the hands of another.

family preservation: A philosophy of child protective services by which parents who have been identified as abusive to their children are provided with intense in-home counseling so that they do not lose their children to foster care.

family violence: Abuse that occurs between family members, including partner to partner or parent to child; it can also occur between siblings and from child to elderly parent.

felony: A crime more serious than a misdemeanor, usually involving use of a weapon or intent to cause severe injury.

foster care: A family with whom a child temporarily lives when removed from the parental home by child protective services; can be short-term or lead to adoption.

harassment: Persistent unwanted attention or repeated threats.

high-risk: People who, because of their circumstances, are more likely to abuse their children or spouse.

home-based services: Postabuse programs run by child protective services to help parents who are at risk of losing their children to foster care improve the situations that led them to abuse their children; in these services, children remain in the home.

home visiting programs: Private or state-sponsored services for high-risk families in which caseworkers visit their homes for intensive counseling in child care and violent behavior management before abuse occurs.

incest: Sexual intercourse between blood relations.

intergenerational violence: Abuse that continues from one generation of a family to another.

intimate violence: Abuse that occurs between people who are close companions or spouses.

kinship care: Foster care provided by a family member other than the abusive caregiver, such as a grandparent.

mandatory arrest policy: Laws that require police officers to arrest an abuser when they strongly suspect that the person has injured another.

miscarriage: The involuntary end of a pregnancy with the death of the fetus.

misdemeanor: A criminal act less serious than a felony; includes illegal shoving, striking, or harassing.

multidisciplinary approach: The practice of utilizing the varied resources of many community groups to address a community problem such as family violence.

multiple abuse: When more than one family member is abused by another.

neglect: Purposeful withholding of nutrition, medical attention, and socialization of a child by a parent.

order of protection: A court order that legally protects a victim of abuse by ordering the abuser to stay away.

permanency planning: Child protective services procedures for finding a permanent home for a child who cannot remain with his or her parents.

physical violence: A deliberate act that causes pain or injury to another.

post-traumatic stress disorder: A psychological reaction common among victims of extreme stress—for example, repeated and unavoidable exposure to attacks—including anxiety, flashbacks, and depression.

pro-arrest policy: Another term for mandatory arrest policy.

psychological violence: Any act, such as threats, verbal abuse, or withholding affection or the company of others, that causes a person to develop serious emotional problems.

PTSD: Post-traumatic stress disorder.

respite care: Temporary foster care.

restraining order: An order of protection.

safe houses: Places where abused people, usually women, can live on a temporary basis in order to escape an abuser; their location is kept secret and can only be found through agencies that work with battered victims.

self-defense theory: A legal defense theory in which an accused murderer claims to have killed an abuser for self-protection after years of abuse.

sexual violence: Forcing a person to perform sex against his or her will.

shelters: The most common term for safe houses.

spouse abuse: Violence that occurs within a marriage; it can be physical or emotional abuse.

stalking: To pursue someone in a threatening way.

therapeutic foster care: Consistent, ongoing care provided by foster parents to children who have emotional problems as a result of abuse.

victimless prosecution: A legal way to bring a domestic abuse case to trial without exposing the victim to the trauma of appearing before his or her abuser.

Organizations
to Contact

The following organizations can be useful resources for further research into family violence. All deal with child abuse, domestic violence, or related aspects of family welfare. Many provide written materials as well as information in response to inquiries.

Battered Women's Justice Project
Battered Women's Justice Center
4032 Chicago Ave. S.
Minneapolis, MN 44507
(800) 903-0111, ext. 1
fax: (612) 824-8965

The project provides training, technical assistance, and other resources in the areas of the criminal justice system's response to domestic violence. It also offers information on battered women's self-defense and how battered women are represented legally.

Children's Defense Fund
Safe Start Campaign
25 E St. NW
Washington, DC 20001
(202) 628-8787
fax: (202) 662-3510

A grassroots movement to help keep children safe and make adults more aware of children's issues. It provides safe havens for children, helps formulate legislation, and runs a public media campaign.

Health Resource Center
San Francisco Family Violence Prevention Fund
383 Rhode Island St., Suite 304
San Francisco, CA 74103-5133
(415) 252-8900
fax: (415) 252-8991

The center provides general information packets designed to strengthen the health care response to domestic violence. It also offers technical assistance and library services to support domestic violence training and program development. Further, it addresses the legal rights of battered immigrant and refugee women.

National Center for Prosecution of Child Abuse
99 Canal Center Plaza, Suite 510
Alexandria, VA 22314
(703) 739-0321
fax: (703) 549-6259

The center works to improve the handling of child abuse cases by providing legal training, information about child abuse case law, publications, and research.

National Clearinghouse for the Defense of Battered Women
125 S. 9th St., Suite 302
Philadelphia, PA 19107
(215) 351-0010

This group provides resources and information to battered women who have killed or assaulted their abusers. It also coordinates a national network of advocates working with women in prison.

National Clearinghouse on Child Abuse and Neglect
PO Box 1182
Washington, DC 20013-1182
(800) FYI-3366
fax: (703) 385-3206

A federal storehouse of data on child abuse that publishes manuals on various aspects of child abuse, including "The Role of Teachers on the Issue of Child Abuse."

National Coalition Against Domestic Violence
PO Box 34103
Washington, DC 20043-4103
(202) 638-6388

The coalition serves as an information and referral center for grassroots shelters and service programs that assist battered women and their children. It also helps other agencies develop programs for battered women.

National Committee to Prevent Child Abuse (NCPCA)
332 S. Michigan Ave., Suite 1600
Chicago, IL 60604
(312) 663-3520
fax: (312) 939-8962

NCPCA serves as a clearinghouse for information about child abuse. It is a nonprofit organization whose mission is to prevent child abuse through advocacy programs, nationwide public information campaigns, workshops, conferences, and research programs. It is the only national organization that compiles an annual survey of child abuse statistics in its "Current Trends in Child Abuse Reporting and Fatalities."

National Council of Juvenile and Family Court Judges
Family Violence Project
University of Nevada
PO Box 8970
Reno, NV 89507
(702) 784-4463
fax: (702) 784-6628

This organization researches and compiles statistics on legal cases involving family violence, with an emphasis on child protection and child custody. It sells a number of publications about the issue of domestic violence. The Family Violence Project is the author of *1994 Family Violence: A Model State Code*, which offers recommendations on how states can handle family violence.

National Resource Center
Pennsylvania Coalition Against Domestic Violence
6400 Flank Dr.
Gateway Corporate Center, Suite 1300
Harrisburg, PA 17112-2778
(800) 537-2238
fax: (717) 545-9456

The center provides information, resources, policy development, and technical assistance to increase awareness of domestic violence and to work toward prevention. Requests for information are handled through voice mail and backlogs can take a few weeks to be filled, but the information is very thorough.

Resolving Conflict Creatively Program (RCCP)
National Center
163 Third Avenue #103
New York, NY 10003
(212) 387-0225
fax: (212) 387-0510

The Resolving Conflict Creatively Program (RCCP), an initiative of Educators for Social Responsibility (ESR), is the largest school-based program in conflict resolution and intergroup relations in the country, serving 325 schools in eight sites nationwide. RCCP equips young people and adults with skills that reduce violence and prejudice and promote caring and cooperative schools and communities.

Suggestions for Further Reading

Gilda Berger, *Violence and the Family.* New York: Franklin Watts, 1990.

William A. Check, *Child Abuse.* New York: Chelsea House, 1989.

Morton L. Kurland, M.D., *Coping with Family Violence.* New York: Rosen Publishing Group, 1986.

Mary Lystad, ed., *Violence in the Home.* New York: Brunner/Mazel, 1986.

Mary Marecek, *Breaking Free from Partner Abuse: Voices of Battered Women Caught in the Cycle of Domestic Violence.* Buena Park, CA: Morning Glory Press, 1993.

Ginny NiCarthy, *The Ones Who Got Away: Women Who Left Abusive Partners.* Seattle: Seal Press, 1987.

Ginny NiCarthy, Karen Merriam, and Sandra Coffman, *Talking It Out.* Seattle: Seal Press, 1984.

Works Consulted

Robert L. Allen and Paul Kivel, "Men Changing Men," *Ms.*, September/October 1994.

American Bar Association Commission on Domestic Violence, *ABA Midyear Meeting Report*, February 9, 1995.

Karen Brandon, "Home Visiting: An Avenue to Stability," *Chicago Tribune*, August 22, 1994.

Karen Brandon and Michael Lev, "Curbing Abuse of Children, a Matter of National Will," *Chicago Tribune*, August 22, 1994.

Rosemary Bray, "Remember the Children," *Ms.*, September/October 1994.

Christiane N. Brown, "New Laws to Protect You from Stalkers," *Good Housekeeping*, August 1993.

Angela Browne, *When Battered Women Kill.* New York: The Free Press, 1987.

Liza N. Burby, "Domestic-Violence Victims Find Understanding," *New York Times*, August 29, 1993.

———, "Natural Helpers Open Student Communication Lines," *Hotline*, Fall 1993.

———, "What's Love Got to Do with It?" *National Council of Jewish Women Journal*, vol. 17, no. 1, fall 1994.

Margaret Carlson, "The Victim You Say?" *Time*, July 4, 1994.

Rosemary Chalk, *Violence and the American Family*. Washington, DC: National Academy Press, 1994.

Howard Davidson, "The Impact of Domestic Violence on Children," *A Report to the President of the American Bar Association*, August 1994.

Jill Davis, "Failure to Protect and Its Impact on Battered Mothers," *Courts and Communities, Confronting Violence in the Family,* vol. 1, no. 3, 1995.

Mary Ann Dutton, "Understanding Women's Response to Domestic Violence: A Redefinition of Battered Women's Syndrome," *Hofstra Law Review*, vol. 21, no. 4, summer 1993.

Charles Patrick Ewing, *When Children Kill: The Dynamics of Juvenile Homicide*. Lexington, MA: D.C. Heath, 1990.

Roger S. Glass, "Keeping the Peace," *American Teacher*, Publication of the American Federation of Teachers AFL-CIO, February 1994.

"Grisly Beating Case Yields First Conviction Under New U.S. Law," *Los Angeles Times*, May 24, 1995.

Jane Gross, "Simpson Case Galvanizes U.S. About Domestic Violence," *New York Times*, July 4, 1994.

Barbara J. Hart, "State Codes on Domestic Violence: Analysis, Commentary, and Recommendations," *Juvenile and Family Court Journal*, vol. 43, no. 4, 1992.

Kathleen M. Heide, *Why Kids Kill Parents*. Columbus: Ohio State University Press, 1992.

Sharon D. Herzberger, *Violence Within the Family: Social Psychological Perspectives*. Madison, WI: Brown & Benchmark, 1996.

Philip J. Hilts, "6% of Women Report Beatings While Pregnant," *New York Times*, March 3, 1994.

Linda Hirshman, "Making Safety a Civil Right," *Ms.*, September/October 1994.

Steven A. Holmes, "G.O.P. Seeks Shift in Child Welfare," *New York Times*, March 13, 1995.

Michele Ingrassia and Melinda Beck, "Patterns of Abuse," *Newsweek*, July 4, 1994.

Gloria Jacobs, "Where Do We Go from Here? An Interview with Ann Jones," *Ms.*, September/October 1994.

Jennifer R. James, "Turning the Tables: Redefining Self-Defense Theory for Children Who Kill Abusive Parents," *Law and Psychology Review*, vol. 18, spring 1994.

Rita Henley Jensen, "A Day in Court," *Ms.*, September/October 1994.

Alexis Jetter, "How Battered Wives Can Learn to Leave," *McCall's*, September 1994.

Ann Jones and Susan Schechter, *When Love Goes Wrong: What to Do When You Can't Do Anything Right*. New York: HarperCollins, 1992.

Rob Karwath, Louise Kiernan, and John W. Fountain, "Adrift in DCFS: Some Kids Can Never Be Saved," *Chicago Tribune*, March 10, 1994.

———, "Child Welfare's Past, a Series of Struggles," *Chicago Tribune*, March 6, 1994.

———, "Fixing DCFS Mess Begins with Basic Steps," *Chicago Tribune*, March 11, 1994.

————, "Fixing Families from Scratch, DCFS Teaches the Basics: Cooking, Cleaning, Proper Care of Children," *Chicago Tribune*, March 8, 1994.

————, "In Search of Remedies, Each Call May Be a Child's Last Hope, Burden Grows on DCFS Hot Line," *Chicago Tribune*, March 6, 1994.

————, "Life or Death in the Balance, Custody Decisions DCFS' Hardest," *Chicago Tribune*, March 7, 1994.

————, "When Kids Need It Most, Foster Families Open Hearts for $10 a Day, It Has to Be for Love," *Chicago Tribune*, March 9, 1994.

Alene Kristal, "You've Come a Long Way, Baby: The Battered Women's Syndrome Revisited," *New York Law School Journal of Human Rights*, vol. 9, fall 1991.

Michael Lev and Karen Brandon, "Intervention May Save Kids from Violence at Home," *Chicago Tribune*, August 21, 1994.

Karen McCurdy, principal analyst, "Current Trends in Child Abuse Reporting and Fatalities: The Results of the 1994 Annual Fifty State Survey." Chicago: National Committee to Prevent Child Abuse, April 1995.

Michael K. Molitor, "The 'Battered Child Syndrome' as Self-Defense Evidence in Parricide Cases: Recent Developments and a Possible Approach," *Wayne Law Review*, vol. 40, fall 1993.

Paul Mones, *When a Child Kills: Abused Children Who Kill Their Parents*. New York: Pocket Books, 1991.

Greggory W. Morris, *The Kids Next Door: Sons and Daughters Who Kill Their Parents*. New York: William Morrow, 1985.

National Clearinghouse for the Defense of Battered Women, *Working Papers, Set #1: July, 1990.*

National Council of Juvenile and Family Court Judges, Advisory Committee, "Model Code on Domestic and Family Violence," 1994.

National Research Council, *Understanding and Preventing Violence*. Washington, DC: National Academy Press, 1993.

——, *Understanding Child Abuse and Neglect*. Washington, DC: National Academy Press, 1993.

——, *Violence in Urban America: Mobilizing a Response*. Washington, DC: National Academy Press, 1994.

Dennis Romero, "Target: Parents," *Los Angeles Times*, March 21, 1995.

Maria Roy, *Children in the Crossfire: Violence in the Home—How Does It Affect Our Children?* Deerfield Beach, FL: Health Communications, Inc., 1988.

Maria Roy, ed. *Battered Women, a Psychosociological Study of Domestic Violence*. New York: Van Nostrand Reinhold, 1977.

Lisbeth B. Schorr, *Within Our Reach: Breaking the Cycle of Disadvantage*. New York: Anchor Press, 1988.

Jill Smolowe, "When Violence Hits Home," *Time*, July 4, 1994.

Karin L. Swisher, Carol Wekesser, and William Barbour, eds., *Violence Against Women*. San Diego: Greenhaven Press, 1994.

Andrew Vachss, "You Carry the Cure in Your Own Heart," *Parade*, August 28, 1994.

Violent Crime Control and Law Enforcement Act of 1994, "Violence Against Women Act," Public Law 103-322, September 13, 1994.

Lenore E. Walker, *The Battered Woman Syndrome*. New York: Springer, 1984.

——, *Terrifying Love: Why Battered Women Kill and How Society Responds*. New York: Harper & Row, 1989.

Sandra Weber, "Long Island Q & A: The Need for Coherent Approaches to Deal with Child Abuse," *New York Times*, April 30, 1995.

Index

About the Author

Liza N. Burby is a book editor and the author of three nonfiction books for young adults, including *World Hunger* for Lucent Books. She has written extensively on the topic of family violence for the *New York Times* and national magazines. She frequently writes articles about other social issues, as well as profiles of interesting people.

Picture Credits

DATE DUE

DEMCO 38-297